VERMONT
MONTPELIER, VT.

WITHDRAWN

WITHDRAWN

Environment and Policies in

West Africa

by R. J. HARRISON CHURCH

Reader in Geography in the University of London
at the London School of Economics and Political Science

A SEARCHLIGHT ORIGINAL
under the general editorship of

GEORGE W. HOFFMAN
University of Texas

G. ETZEL PEARCY
United States
Department of State

D. VAN NOSTRAND COMPANY, INC.
PRINCETON, NEW JERSEY

TORONTO   LONDON

NEW YORK

D. VAN NOSTRAND COMPANY, INC.
120 Alexander St., Princeton, New Jersey
(*Principal Office*)
24 West 40 Street, New York 18, New York

D. VAN NOSTRAND COMPANY, LTD.
358, Kensington High Street, London, W.14, England

D. VAN NOSTRAND COMPANY (Canada), LTD.
25 Hollinger Road, Toronto 16, Canada

―――――――

COPYRIGHT © 1963, BY
D. VAN NOSTRAND COMPANY, INC.

―――――――

Published simultaneously in Canada by
D. VAN NOSTRAND COMPANY (Canada), LTD.

―――――――

No reproduction in any form of this book, in whole or in part (except for brief quotation in critical articles or reviews), may be made without written authorization from the publishers

―――――――

PRINTED IN THE UNITED STATES OF AMERICA

916.6
C562e

Preface

West Africa is one of the most vigorously developing areas of the world, and certainly of Africa. Politically, it was transformed from almost complete colonialism in early 1957 to all but entire freedom by early 1961. Economically, it is a major world producer and seller of cocoa (two-thirds of world production), palm kernels (three-quarters), palm oil (one-third), peanuts and derivatives (one-third), diamonds (one-third by weight), and manganese (one-fifth). Large hydroelectric power projects may transform Ghana, Nigeria, and Guinea, and the Volta River Project should make Ghana into a leading producer of aluminum.

West Africa is very much on the world map, as well as having recently remade its own map. This study outlines the relations of the area and its diverse countries in the setting of their physical and economic environments.

After defining West Africa and outlining its importance, the first chapter describes the evolution of the map from the earliest times to the present day from a geographical viewpoint. The countries are collectively and individually surveyed in Chapter 2, with particular reference to their historical backgrounds, geographical characteristics, economy, political situation, and policies. More space has been given to the lesser known countries.

Old colonial groupings and allegiances have been broken and there are now 13 independent states, several with small areas or low populations, all with poor standards of living. Present political loyalties, one-party rule, Negritude, the African personality, and Pan-Africanism are discussed in Chapter 3, as well as the Ghana-Guinea-Mali Union (Union of African States) and the Benin-Sahel Entente.

Survival and progress, however, depend upon improving agri-

3

15/63

culture and livestock; the mining of minerals; the development of industry, power, transportation, and commerce; and the diversification of economies. Much also depends upon types of association with the European Economic Community, and upon the development of trade within Africa, reviewed in Chapter 4. Finally, the concluding chapter discusses West Africa's relationships with other countries, including the United States and European, Asian, and other African lands, as well as with the United Nations.

I am honored to have been asked to contribute to this fine series. My sincerest thanks go to my typist, the editors, cartographers, publisher, and printers for their help. May this book contribute to an understanding of one of the world's most lively areas.

R. J. HARRISON CHURCH

The London School of
Economics and Political Science
January, 1963

Contents

List of Maps

I *The Evolution of*
the Present Map

WEST AFRICA is a well-defined part of Africa. Desert separates it from North Africa, and the Cameroon, Bamenda, and Adamawa mountains keep it apart from the very different lowland West Central Africa. The Atlantic washes its coasts, which are more southern than western.

The vast and compact continent of Africa occupies 11.7 million square miles; of this, West Africa covers 2.4 million square miles, or one-fifth. Yet its population of 70 million is 30 per cent of that of all Africa. West Africa is thus well-populated by African standards. It has been in contact with Europe and the rest of the world for a longer period than any other area of Africa, except for the ancient links of Mediterranean Africa with Asia.

West Africa, however, is more appropriately compared with the rest of Tropical Africa, of which it occupies 30 per cent of the area, has 40 per cent of the population, and nearly 40 per cent of the external trade. It has some very large clusters of population, particularly in Western and Eastern Nigeria, the former having Tropical Africa's largest city—Ibadan. External trade in crops is more developed than in most parts of Tropical Africa, and mineral production is advancing rapidly.

From west to east, West Africa extends as far as from San Francisco to New York, or from London to Moscow, and its area is some five-sixths that of the United States.

Nine republics formerly administered by France occupy three-quarters of the area. However, about half their total area is

7

Saharan, and they have little more than one-third of West Africa's population. By contrast, Nigeria, fourth most populated country of the British Commonwealth, has nearly one-half the population of West Africa; indeed, one in seven Africans is a Nigerian.

Nature presents vivid contrasts, mainly between the south, and the north or interior. The former, which has a higher rainfall that is more evenly distributed throughout the year, has a long growing season and the greatest agricultural potential, although the soils may be severely leached in the southwestern areas of heaviest rainfall. Areas south of about 8°N that were originally forested—and often still are—may provide timber and can sustain valuable tree crops such as the oil palm, cocoa, coffee, rubber, kola, and bananas, as well as varied food crops from tubers such as manioc (cassava), corn (maize), and rice. The mainly negro peoples were formerly organized in usually small societies, although the Ashanti developed a wider confederacy. Originally Animist, these peoples are now often Christian, and as the result of some four centuries of contact with Europe they are much westernized, especially in towns.

By contrast, the northern and interior drier areas have a shorter rainy season and therefore much more restricted agricultural possibilities, although the soils are less leached. These areas, originally covered by woodland that was thinnest and shortest toward the desert, are now almost entirely savannah zones. Cash crops are necessarily fewer, because of the shorter growing season and greater distance from ports and markets; peanuts and cotton are the main cash crops. Food crops are mostly cereals, particularly millets and sorghum (guinea corn). Nevertheless, alongside the more restricted agricultural range, there is a separate pastoral economy operated by nomads who keep cattle more for subsistence and prestige than for sale, and who grow almost no crops. Most of the nomads and many of the fixed agriculturalists are Islamic; the former have tended to rule the latter. It is in this part of West Africa that most of the states of the past were located.

The earliest states were situated around the upper and middle Niger river and between it and Lake Chad. Despite the long dry season of 8 to 9 months, and an annual rainfall of never more than 40 inches (more commonly around 20 inches and highly variable), their woodland or savannah environments provided an open landscape. This facilitated movement, as did the rivers and the horse which could be used here because of the absence of the tsetse fly. Ghana flourished north of the upper Niger from the eighth to thirteenth centuries, Mali succeeded it and flourished around the upper Niger and the Bani tributary until the sixteenth century, and Songhay, centered on Gao, was partly contemporaneous with Mali. The Hausa states developed east of Songhay from the eleventh century onward, as did Bornu around Lake Chad.

Economic development within these many states mainly depended upon the occurrence of sufficient surface water from rivers or underground water from wells for men, animals, and crops. Gold was mined in Bambouk, between the Faléme and Bafing headwaters of the Senegal (now on the border between the Senegal and Mali Republics).

Above all, these states flourished through trans-Saharan trade. They were most fortunately located between the Sahara and the West African forest lands that were their frontiers for further sources of gold—in what is now the Ivory Coast, modern Ghana, and Nigeria—slaves, ivory, and spices. Gold, ivory, and spices were in demand in Europe and were important trade items between Arabs (who received them in North Africa from across the desert) and traders from the Venetian and Genoese republics. Slaves were then destined for the Arab world. Important to West Africa was salt dug in the Sahara, European cloth, and other luxuries obtained by the Arabs from the Venetians and Genoese.

Many ancient cities derived their significance from trans-Saharan trade. Most were sited on the edge of the desert, for example, Walata of ancient Ghana, Timbuktu of Mali, Gao of Songhay, Kano of one of the Hausa states, and Hadejia and Kukwa of Bornu. Some of these and many others have decayed with the decline of trans-Saharan trade, others have lingered on like Timbuktu, and some have revived, like Gao and Kano, as the termini of new routes.

Following the Moroccan conquest of Songhay in 1591, there was no dominant political unit in the savannah zone, but rather an aggregation of minor states. Moreover, the Ottoman Turkish conquest of North Africa severely curtailed trans-Saharan trade and thus cut at the roots of the economy of the savannah zone. Political and economic decay set in until revived in the nineteenth century under French colonial rule.

On the other hand, as the savannah states declined, the powerful Ashanti, Dahomey, Yoruba, and Benin states were developing in the forest zone. The advent of the Portuguese, Dutch, Swedes, Danes, Brandenburgers, French, and English to the Guinea coast diverted remaining trade from across the desert to routes through the forest and Guinea coastal points. Space relationships, therefore, were utterly reversed—the interior decayed whereas the coastal areas prospered.

However, the soon-dominant slave trade greatly upset African societies. Domestic slavery was not new in Africa; indeed, it is not unknown even now. Nor was it first commercialized by Europeans for, as we have just seen, it was a vital element in the Arab trans-Saharan caravans. Moreover, whereas Arabs were engaged in the trade for about a thousand years, especially in northern, north-eastern, eastern, and east-central Africa, Europeans engaged in it for less than one-third that period. On the other hand, they engaged in it more intensively through the West African and West Central coasts of the continent. It is possible that 20 million people were removed from West Africa, and up to 50 million from all Africa.

Many studies have been made of the effects of the slave trade upon Africa, the consequences of which are still to be seen. In West Africa vast areas were depopulated by slave raiding, by the fear of being taken into slavery, or by the population being so decimated that the tsetse fly could not be controlled and thus spread sleeping sickness, bringing death to the survivors from slavery. The Middle Belt, between about 8°N and 11°N in West (and West Central Africa) was thus depopulated by Arab slave raiders from the north and by agents of European slavers from the south. It remains a problem area to this day.

African societies were fragmented and broken up by their leaders being captured, and by raiding one another for prisoners to be sold into slavery. Political, social, and economic conditions degenerated, and all Arabs and Europeans were viewed with suspicion for a long time.

The main incidental benefit that Africa received from the slave trade was the introduction by the Portuguese of American crops whose produce would keep well, and could be used for feeding captives on the long Atlantic crossing. Thus, manioc (cassava), sweet potatoes, peanuts, corn (maize), lima beans, and chillies were introduced.

The American continents' demand for slaves brought negroes to the New World, introduced a racial problem to the United States, and changed the racial composition of most West Indian islands. Brazil has absorbed its negroes with outward harmony and official equality. Tribal customs have been transplanted. In Dutch Guiana, negroes maintain a way of life brought by their slave ancestors from Ashanti through Dutch slaving castles in West Africa; Dahomey ceremonies can be seen in Haiti and Yoruba ones in Brazil. Jazz is a negro gift to modern civilization. During four centuries West Africa was despoiled for the development of the Americas and the enrichment of Europe.

Abolition of the slave trade—first by Denmark; secondly, and far more importantly, by Great Britain—led to new forms of contact with West Africa as atonement for the trade. Settlements were created in and around Freetown, in what later became British Sierra Leone, for slaves freed from Britain, the United States, Jamaica, and slave ships. Likewise, many settlements were made along the Grain Coast by the American Colonization Society and other societies of slaves from the United States, and slaves freed from slave ships by the American Navy. In 1847, Liberia became independent; its motto became "The Love of Liberty Brought Us Here." Thus, Sierra Leone and Liberia have similar origins.

European interest in West Africa as such (as, indeed, in Tropical Africa as a whole) became considerable only in the last quarter of the nineteenth century, four centuries later than European maritime contact with Asia and the Americas, all more productive of trade than Africa.

Several economic factors led to the interest in Africa for its own sake—the need to develop legitimate trade to compensate both Africans and Europeans for losses consequent upon the abolition of the slave trade, the need for tropical vegetable oils to lubricate machinery of the new industrial era then almost ignorant of mineral-oil lubricants, and the need for candles (then an important illuminant) and soap for the mounting industrial populations then being converted to the virtues of frequent washing.

The precipitating political factor was the Conference of Berlin's doctrine that political title to territory in Africa could only be sustained by effective occupancy. French penetration, the earliest and most systematic, followed the relatively easy route of the navigable Senegal river, down that of the Niger, and overland toward Lake Chad, as well as inland from the southern Guinea coast. The general object was to restore prestige lost by defeat in the Franco-Prussian war of 1870-71. The particular object was to link French possessions in North, West, West Central, and Northeast Africa (Obok, later French Somaliland). The last link was frustrated in 1898, but the others succeeded—albeit at the cost of France ruling over much desert and otherwise poor areas.

British penetration was hesitant and selective. Under Gladstone, Britain sought no colonial advance; indeed, withdrawal was often recommended. Under Disraeli, advance was encouraged, but for strictly limited purposes. Lagos was taken to stop the slave trade still centered there. Much of the rest of Nigeria was taken to transfer political administration from a private company, the Royal Niger Company, as well as to offset French and German penetration all around. Advance in the then Gold Coast was precipitated by Ashanti attacks on coastal peoples, and farther north by French

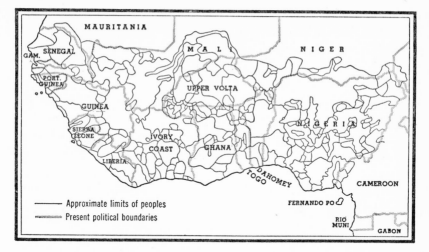

Figure 1   The Main Peoples of West Africa—The Pre-Colonial Political Map (Simplified from maps of L. Pales, *Mission Anthropologique,* Dakar, 1949, and *Géographie Universelle Larousse,* Vol. 2, 1959, pp. 120-121)

movement, as it was into the interior of Sierra Leone by French penetration on the north and east.

The intricate mosaic of indigenous West Africa, broadly portrayed in Figure 1, received an overlay of colonial political units, consisting of continuous French territory and inter-digitations of one Portuguese, one German, and four British possessions. Portuguese Guinea is a relic reminder of former Portuguese interests, mainly in the slave trade, all along the coast. German Togo was conquered during World War I and divided into larger French and smaller British League of Nations Mandates, both of which were transformed after World War II into United Nations Trusteeships.

The establishment of mandates and of the League of Nations Mandates Commission after World War I was the first evidence of international concern with colonies, albeit former colonies of defeated Germany and Turkey. The National Congress of British West Africa held in 1922 was the first evidence of a movement thinking toward independence and Pan-Africanism. It was, however, World War II that hastened the spread of African nationalism. British African volunteers served in Southeast Asia, and French African conscripts served in Europe, North Africa, and Southeast Asia. British West Africa was an important reception and transit area for American supplies that were mainly destined for the North African Front. In 1943, French West Africa, changing its allegiance from Vichy to the Allies, fulfilled the same function, especially through its great port, airport, federal capital, and nerve center of Dakar.

Since at least 1922, British colonial policy had provided for eventual independence, and mainly-lowland British West Africa had been saved from the difficulties of highland white settler countries by the mosquito. It was also saved by enlightened administrators, and by fairly dense populations in Nigeria and the then southern Gold Coast from the granting of freehold land to non-African individuals and companies.

Leader in the movement for independence in British West Africa was the Gold Coast, richest of the four colonies and the most homogeneous; equally important was Nigeria, but her size and diversity required the more complicated evolution through federal government to independence. In 1951, Dr. Nkrumah was released from prison, and his sentence for sedition, to become Leader of Government Business as the chief of the Convention Peoples Party that had just won an election. In 1954, he became Prime Minister, and in 1957, the Gold Coast with the United Kingdom Trusteeship of Togo became independent Ghana.

In Nigeria, parliaments were established in each Region in 1946, and these were given greater powers in 1951. Regionalization went further in 1954; Western and Eastern Nigeria became self-governing in 1957, Northern Nigeria in 1959, and the whole Federation of Nigeria became fully independent in 1960.

Sierra Leone was for long too poor and was thought to be unduly small for independence; however, extensive African digging of diamonds has brought remarkable wealth, and Sierra Leone became independent in 1961. Independence "in one form or another" has been promised to the tiny Gambia.

Until 1944 French policy had been one of *Assimilation,* of governing her territories in such a way that they would ultimately become overseas departments of France. This was completely opposed to British aims of eventual independence and, whereas the British sought to safeguard indigenous life and institutions, the French preferred to eliminate them or assimilate them to French ones. Education was mostly in French, and textbooks were identical with those in France. By contrast, leaders in ex-British West Africa have often been educated in their own traditions or in the non-West African and non-British tradition in the United States. Instead of a color bar there was a cultural rift between *citizens* who had assimilated French culture and had the right to vote, and *subjects* who had neither. The former were accepted like metropolitan French, and there were many mixed marriages. Citizens formed the elite, and politicians spent most of their time in Paris since they were elected to the French Chamber of Deputies, local parliaments then having only advisory powers except over the budget.

In 1944, at the Brazzaville Conference organized by the Free French, a new policy of *Association* was defined. Instead of hoping to create French Africans, the emphasis was now on producing African Frenchmen. More respect was paid to indigenous customs, all inhabitants became citizens, and forced labor was abolished. French policy moved toward the British, and General de Gaulle was identified in many African peoples' minds as a colonial reformer.

French West Africa was much influenced by the events outlined above in British West Africa and by nationalist movements in Morocco and Tunisia, and French Indo-China. It was also much affected by dislike of the intense centralization of government through the peripheral federal capital of Dakar and even more so in Paris. Such centralized government contrasted strongly with the very decentralized government always practiced in British colonies.

Short-lived French governments with bare majorities and odd

bed-fellows in unstable coalitions were not able to make reforms
until the *Loi Cadre* (outline law) of 1956. This provided a framework within which each territory could develop its own political
institutions, with ministerial government, its own laws, and eventual
self-government.

Assimilation and its kindred Association were boldly replaced by
a policy providing for local autonomy, not far short of the British
policy of eventual independence. These changes had barely been
made when the Fourth Republic collapsed and General de Gaulle
returned to power.

In September, 1958, a referendum was taken in France and her
overseas territories concerning the new constitution for France and
for the French Community, within which France and the autonomous overseas members would jointly decide foreign policy, defense,
currency, economic policies, higher education, and pensions. Of the
eight French West African countries, seven chose to be autonomous
states of the community; Guinea alone said "no" and was given
highly cold-shouldered independence. Because of their friendship
with France, the Western powers did not hasten to help Guinea
and this, combined with the radicalism of Guinea's president Sekou
Touré, presented the Communist powers with a wide open door.
Ghana also helped Guinea with a loan of $28 million, technical and
administrative assistance, and an agreement to form a Union with
Guinea. This association (for such it has seemed to be, rather than
a union) was the first across the old colonial boundaries.

This was the initial rent in the Federation of French West Africa.
The second was between those in Senegal like Leopold Senghor and
in the then Soudan like Modibo Keita, who wished to retain the
advantages of federation by regrouping self-governing republics
within the French Community. The formation of the new Federation of Mali was announced in January, 1959, supported by the above
two republics, the Upper Volta, and Dahomey. The last two dropped
out before the Federation was legally constituted in mid-1959, and
even the two-state Federation of Mali collapsed a year later when the
Sudanese and Federal Prime Minister, Modibo Keita, put himself

forward as presidential candidate, despite an understanding that the President should be Senegalese. Senegal then seceded from the Mali Federation, which thus collapsed, and the Sudanese Republic became the Mali Republic. Shortly after, Mali joined the Ghana-Guinea Union, now officially known as the Union of African States.

Meanwhile, most leaders in the successor republics of former French West Africa wished for a separate agreement by each republic with the Community. They were understandably led by M. Houphouët-Boigny, Prime Minister of the Ivory Coast, the richest country of former French West Africa, and far away from the hated centralization of Dakar. In May, 1959, he formed the Benin-Sahel Entente, a political and economic association of the naturally close Ivory Coast, Upper Volta, Niger, and Dahomey, a counterpoise to the Mali Federation, the far stronger Ghana, the Ghana-Guinea Union, and to Nigeria.

In December, 1959, the six-months old Mali Federation (and Madagascar) obtained from General de Gaulle the agreement that countries could become completely independent, and yet remain within the French Community. This came about for the countries named in June, 1960. The Mali Federation broke up soon after, and Senegal has alone remained within the Community, a Commonwealth of Nations *à la française*. De Gaulle had appreciated the need to concede independence; what Guinea had secured in mutual recrimination in 1958, the Mali Federation and Madagascar secured by sweet reasonableness in 1959-60.

Full independence was infectious. M. Houphouët-Boigny, a staunch francophile, who scorned full independence for years, had to demand it in July, 1960, for the four partners of the Benin-Sahel Entente. Mali had achieved independence within the French Community, Ghana three years earlier in the British Commonwealth, and Nigeria was to achieve it. Guinea, thrown out into the cold was soon the subject of warm embraces from the East and later from the West. What others had achieved, M. Houphouët-Boigny was bound to ask to retain his following in his own country and the continued association of the Upper Volta, Niger, and Dahomey in the Benin-Sahel Entente. The four partners became independent in August, 1960. Mauritania, then the poorest land of West Africa, followed in November, 1960, the last republic of former French West Africa to do so. The French Trusteeship of Togo had ended in April, 1960, when the country became independent. Nigeria became independent in October, 1960, and Sierra Leone in April, 1961.

Thus, from 1847 to 1957, Liberia was the only sovereign independent state in the modern sense of the word in West Africa, and for much of that time her freedom was precarious. Ghana became the second independent state in 1957, Guinea the third in 1958, and the rest followed in 1960, except for Sierra Leone in 1961. Only

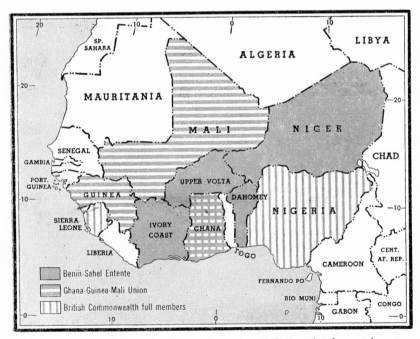

Figure 2   West Africa and Adjacent Countries, 1962. Associated countries are Ivory Coast, Upper Volta, Niger, and Dahomey in the Benin-Sahel Entente; the Ghana-Guinea-Mali Union; and the British Commonwealth full members—Nigeria, Ghana, Sierra Leone

Portuguese Guinea and the Gambia then remained under European rule.

The huge Federation of French West Africa has been replaced by eight separate republics, four that are associated in the Benin-Sahel Entente, and two that are associated with Ghana in the Union of African States. (See Figure 2.) Ghana became a republic, largely to clarify her independence, and this is likely to happen in time to Nigeria and Sierra Leone. Lastly, the Southern Cameroons voted in 1961 to join the Republic of Cameroon (ex-French Trusteeship, French spelling *Cameroun*) and did so on a federal basis as Western Cameroon, the rest of the Republic of Cameroon being renamed Eastern Cameroon. Other parts of the United Kingdom Trusteeship of the Cameroons voted to join Nigeria, and did so as the Sardauna Province of Northern Nigeria.

In four years the political map of West Africa has been utterly transformed and, alas, Balkanized. The federal agencies of research, transportation, etc., of the former Federation of French West Africa have been territorialized. West Africa now has 13 independent states, many of which are under-populated, undersized, and far too poor to be able to survive with their own resources.

The well-populated, large, and diversely endowed Nigeria plainly stands apart, although its federal structure has been and will continue to be subjected to great strains. Its survival depends upon human give and take and good statesmanship; for most of the others it seems to depend upon long-continuing foreign aid.

Furthermore, the consequences of colonial policies and theories—political, economic, and social—largely remain and will long remain as credits and debits, as they have in all other former colonial countries, be they ex-Roman Britain or ex-British America.

West Africa has had two main imprints—French and British. Three-quarters of the area has French as its only common and official language, one-quarter (but two-thirds of the people) has English. External, albeit international, languages have been superimposed upon the indigenous linguistic structure, facilitating communication within each state, and between it and speakers of the same language elsewhere in the world, but making West African unity more difficult, at least until both languages are understood by most of the elite throughout West Africa. Great efforts are being made to have both languages taught to all secondary school children in West Africa.

Each country has been given a modern administrative structure and organization, modeled more or less upon that of the former metropolitan power, and more or less suited to the West African country in question. The ex-French countries have inherited a highly centralized system, the ex-British highly decentralized ones. Local temperaments and political ideals may modify these. Thus, Ghana has become more centralized; and if Communist influence grows in Guinea, the administrative and economic structure may change still more in spirit and in method.

Nationalism was born of the struggle against colonial rule. But it was an "ad hoc" nationalism, superimposed upon the tribal one, and limited to the area within the colonial boundaries. One of the vital questions for the future is whether loyalties will now be mainly tribal or mainly national; even more, whether public opinion can encourage technical cooperation or political integration across boundaries.

Boundaries in West Africa are very often geometrical and superimposed upon earlier settlements, frequently dividing peoples between two countries. Thus the Ewe and the Hausa have had very different political, social, and economic systems imposed upon them according to which side of the line they found themselves.

At the beginning of colonial rule, the French stripped the chiefs of all but ceremonial functions, whereas the British retained the chiefs in all their powers so long as these were compatible with civilized conceptions. By safeguarding the rights and privileges of chiefs as they found them around 1900, the British often fossilized the framework they found and protected. Moreover, in some societies where chiefs were unknown, as among the Ibo in southeastern Nigeria, considerable efforts were made to create them and to get them accepted. The new political leaders and the traditional chiefs have often looked askance at each other, as in Ghana. Furthermore, elective forms of local government may be difficult to introduce, since they may throw up leaders different from and even antagonistic to chiefs—this has been the case in Northern Nigeria. Here also women had not been given the vote by 1961 because the Islamic Emirs were averse to it; although across the boundary, in the more overwhelmingly Islamic Niger Republic, women had the vote for several years, because the French had decreed it under colonial rule, and had long ago reduced their Emirs to powerless figureheads.

In education the consequences are very evident to the student of international affairs, especially if he attends an international conference. The leaders of ex-French West Africa have all the eloquence of French speakers, and some, like Senghor, are authors of world renown. They have spoken French from childhood, as long as French people of the same age, and their education stressed the importance of accurate written and especially verbal exposition and logic. In Britain this is stressed only in the so-called Public (in fact very Private) Schools, attended by few Africans, and whose influence on education in British West Africa was almost confined to Achimota College, near Accra, Ghana. This was attended by some of Ghana's leaders, whose public declarations are notably eloquent.

Economic development and trade also proceeded according to very contrasted policies, as explained in Chapter 4. White emigration to French colonies was permitted, and land could be obtained freehold. In the ex-French republics, the small European trader and café or restaurant owner is common, as is the European shop assistant and *maître d'hôtel*. In the ex-British lands, large British companies and large and small Lebanese traders are common.

West Africa belongs to many trading blocs and financial systems: the Sterling Area with the Nigerian Pound, the Ghana Pound, and the West African Pound (for Sierra Leone and the Gambia) with modest Commonwealth preference; the Franc Zone with the C.F.A. Franc (*Communanté Financière Africaine*) with close links with

France, high guaranteed prices for the most important exports, and great tariff preference for French imports; the Guinea and Mali Franc areas doing much barter trade with the Communist countries; the Dollar area of Liberia that uses American money; and the Escudo area of Portuguese Guinea that has a mercantilist trade relationship with Portugal. It is the existence of these different currencies (often not readily convertible into one another), monetary areas, and trading blocs that has restricted technical cooperation and, still more, political integration across the colonially-determined boundaries. It is precisely these difficulties that have limited the significance of the Union of African States (the Ghana-Guinea-Mali Union).

Production and commerce have depended, and still depend, not only upon the character of the environment—what can be grown, raised, mined, or manufactured—but upon political principles, social attitudes, and economic controls of the colonial past and present, and their legacies.

II   *The Countries of West Africa*

WEST AFRICA has 15 political divisions on the mainland, 13 are independent states and 2 are dependent territories—the Gambia and Portuguese Guinea. Five have English as their official language—the 3 Commonwealth countries of Nigeria, Ghana, and Sierra Leone, and also Liberia and the Gambia. Nine have French as their official language—the 8 former members of French West Africa: Guinea, Senegal, Mauritania, Mali, Upper Volta, Niger, the Ivory Coast, and Dahomey. The ninth is Togo, formerly a French Trusteeship. Portuguese Guinea completes the jigsaw pattern on the mainland. In the Bight of Benin are the Spanish overseas province of Fernando Po, comprising the island of Fernando Po and the islet of Annobon, and the Portuguese overseas province of São Tomé and Príncipe. Off the western point of West Africa are the Cape Verde Islands, another Portuguese overseas province. Table 1 gives the latest available statistics of area and population.

These countries group themselves, or stand apart, in many different ways—for example, geographically, politically, and economically. Taking only the independent countries, they range in size from Togo to the nearly 21 times larger Niger whose population is little more than twice as much; or to Mali, 21 times as large as Togo but with a population less than 3 times greater; or to Mauritania, 19 times larger with only three-quarters the population of Togo. Plainly, the large northern countries have small

23

TABLE 1   West African Countries by Area and Population

Country	Capital	Area in square miles	Population	Date	Density per square mile
Spanish Sahara	El Aïun	102,703	25,000	1959(E)	0.2
Mauritania	Nouakchott	419,121	850,000	1961(E)	2.0
Mali	Bamako	464,752	4,470,000	1961(E)	10.0
Upper Volta	Ouagadougou	105,811	4,160,000	1961(E)	38.0
Niger	Niamey	458,874	3,100,000	1961(E)	6.5
Senegal	Dakar	76,104	3,100,000	1961(E)	39.2
Gambia	Bathurst	4,008	284,000	1960(E)	71.0
Cape Verde Is.	Praia	1,557	201,549	1960(C)	129.4
Portuguese Guinea	Bissau	13,948	544,184	1960(C)	39.0
São Tomé & Príncipe	São Tomé	372	63,676	1960(C)	171.7
Fernando Po & Annobon	Santa Isabel	791	41,878	1950(C)	53.0
Guinea	Conakry	94,901	2,900,000	1961(E)	29.5
Sierra Leone	Freetown	27,925	2,400,000	1959(E)	86.0
Liberia	Monrovia	37,392	750,000	1956(E)	20.1
Ivory Coast	Abidjan	124,471	3,200,000	1961(E)	24.8
Ghana	Accra	91,843	6,726,815	1960(C)	73.4
Togo	Lomé	22,002	1,470,000	1961(E)	66.5
Dahomey	Porto-Novo	44,684	2,080,000	1961(E)	45.0
Nigeria	Lagos	356,669	33,663,000	1959(E)	94.4
Total	—	2,447,928	70,030,102	—	28.6

E = Estimate
C = Census

populations because much, even most, of their areas are desert. Almost all of their peoples and their economy (except mining) are found south of 17°N. Even there, economic possibilities are strictly limited by drought for more than half the year. Mauritania, Mali, and the Niger are mostly either desert or the poorest, dry pasture land. Mauritania has rich iron deposits as compensation, and Mali has the life-giving Niger valley—a lesser Nile that the Niger Republic also enjoys to a small extent.

Senegal and the Upper Volta are small and dry, but less dry countries than the foregoing. Both, but especially Senegal, find their main cash asset in peanuts. Moreover, Senegal has a fortunate situation at the most western point of Africa, and as the nearest tropical land to Europe. Her geographical position has given her great historical and economic significance totally denied, in modern times at least, to the Upper Volta.

The Upper Volta, Mali, and the Niger are the three landlocked states of West Africa dependent upon the Ivory Coast, Ghana, Dahomey, and Nigeria for the transit of their vital overseas trade. Nearly a half of West Africa is occupied by these three landlocked states, but they have less than one-fifth the people of West Africa and only one-thirtieth of its foreign trade.

The lands that lie in zones of past or present forest are those that have the greatest agricultural possibilities and, as they have coast lines, are far more accessible to markets and suppliers. Accessibility to the outside world has also facilitated the development of their important mineral resources, industrial development through processing of exports, and the assembly of imported materials. Because these goods are cheapest near the point of entry, commerce flourishes, especially since most of West Africa's peoples are clustered here and their standard of living is higher than in most inland areas.

Four countries stand out concerning the variety of their resources—mineral and agricultural—and in the development of industries, namely, Guinea, the Ivory Coast, Ghana, and Nigeria. Guinea, however, has a rugged terrain, costly transportation, and an economic system that does not encourage individual initiative. The Ivory Coast has a rather low total population (3.2 million) and density (25 per square mile). Ghana's internal politics have sometimes caused concern. Nigeria, already the giant and with the largest area of productive and diverse country, has nearly half the West African population. In 1957, Guinea had nearly 3 per cent of West Africa's external trade, the Ivory Coast 10 per cent, Ghana 22 per cent, and Nigeria 33 per cent. West Africa accounts for well over one-third of Africa's overseas trade.[1] Internal trade figures are

[1] Hance, William A., Kotschar, Vincent, and Peteerc, Richard J., "Source Areas of Export Production in Tropical Africa," *Geographical Review,* Vol.LI (1961), pp.487-499.

few and unreliable, but Nigeria would undoubtedly stand highest in West Africa.

West African lands have aligned themselves in different ways politically. There is the Benin-Sahel Entente of the Ivory Coast, the Upper Volta, Niger and Dahomey, a conservative association of countries with common constitutions, electoral laws, administrative methods, and economic policy. Another group is the Ghana-Guinea-Mali Union, a link between radicals, which is intended as the nucleus of a wider political union. These three countries are associated with Morocco, Algeria, and Egypt in the Casablanca group of states. These countries believe in political integration, whereas the rest, ex-British and ex-French, are known as the Monrovia group, and believe in technical cooperation as the first step to political integration.

Reference has already been made in Chapter 1 to the different currency zones and world trading blocs to which West African countries are linked. West Africa will remain divided so long as all currencies are not freely convertible, and different tariff systems impede free trade inside West Africa and to and from the rest of the world. Language differences reinforce the barriers. However, different currencies are not entirely the result of, nor, perhaps, even mainly the consequence of colonial rule, for each country would have had to adopt a currency and the result could have been even more varied and divisive.

A. LANDS OF THE SAHARA AND ITS FRINGES

SPANISH SAHARA—ARID RELIC OF AN EMPIRE

The Spanish Sahara is a Spanish overseas province on the African mainland southeast of the Canary Islands. Although entirely desert, it has the luxury of two administrative divisions. The southern division, Rio de Oro, with its capital at Villa Cisneros, has approximately 14,000 almost wholly nomadic inhabitants. The northern division, Saquia-el-Hamra, with its capital (also the general capital) at El Aïun, has approximately 11,000 inhabitants.

The Spanish live in a few fortified settlements, having little contact with the nomadic inhabitants. The Mauritanian iron-ore railroad from Fort Gouraud to Port Etienne could have been built much more cheaply across the southeastern corner of the country, but Spanish terms were so onerous that this was impossible. Yet, a route across part of Spanish Sahara might have helped oil prospection there, been the means for distributing water, and helped development generally. The Spanish Government, however, has granted extensive oil prospecting permits along the Moroccan border and tapering southwest toward Villa Cisneros, as well as licenses to prospect for iron ore, phosphates, and uranium in the interior. (See Figure 3.) Otherwise, it previously did little else other than encourage coastal fishing by Canary Islanders.

If minerals are not located in commercial quantities, and if Morocco and Spain ever did engage in a deal against Mauritania and France, Spain might find it useful to cede Spanish Sahara to Morocco, which claims it as well as Mauritania and western Algeria. Spain did cede the former Southern Spanish Protectorate of Morocco between the Wadi Draa and latitude 27°40′N to Morocco in 1958. If further cession ever occurred it might make Mauritania's independence even more difficult, as well as French support of it.

MAURITANIA—"A BRIDGE BETWEEN WHITE AND BLACK AFRICA"

The quotation from Moktar Ould Daddah, Prime Minister of Mauritania, is a summary of the position occupied by his country. Known officially as the Islamic Republic of Mauritania, it is as large as Texas and California combined, or twice as large as France, yet it has well under one million people, many of whom are nomadic and most of whom are a mixture of some Arab with mostly Berber stock. In 1960 only 6 towns at the most had over 3,000 people. Two-thirds is desert; only along the southern boundary is there extensive cultivable land, even there possible only as annual floods of the Senegal River retreat. Until recently such cultivation as took place there, and in the rare oases, was undertaken by negro slaves. Salt has been cut for centuries from deposits near the center of the coast and near Fort Gouraud in the northwest. (See Figure 3.)

The Almoravids, or reforming Berbers, moved into Morocco from Mauritania to found Marrakech in 1062, and Fez in 1069. They entered Spain in 1083 and advanced to Saragossa, their northern limit from which they later withdrew. Since then most Mauritanians

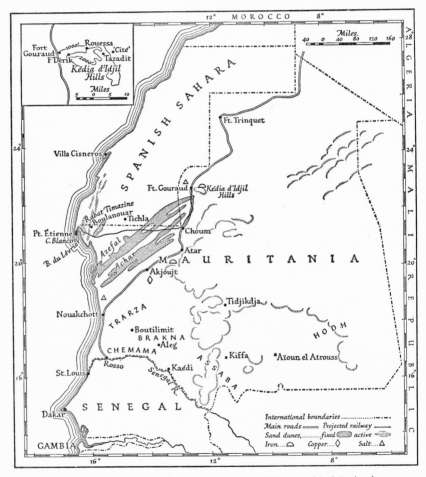

Figure 3   Mauritania (By permission, Royal Geographical Society)

have been organized in nomadic tribes. In the days of considerable trans-Saharan trade between the Arab provinces of North Africa, and Ghana and Mali, gold from Bambouk, negro slaves, and goat skins passed through what is now Mauritania.

The earliest European contact was by the Portuguese, who in 1461 founded a fort on Arguin island, where water was available on an otherwise desert coast. At first, slaves, diverted from the desert caravans, were traded, and, soon after, gum arabic. For some two centuries this was the major source of supply of slaves until, in the late nineteenth century, the Sudan dominated the trade. Mâquil Arabs also entered the country in the sixteenth century, and to them is due the pure Arabic still spoken. The French occupied the country from the south between 1902 and 1914, at a time when they were occupying Morocco in the north. Mauritania became a separate colony only in 1920, and independence came in 1960.

Although the foregoing history might suggest a contrary claim, Morocco has claimed Mauritania on the basis of religious and tribal allegiance of Mauritanian Emirs to the King of Morocco, for whom prayers are said in Mauritanian mosques. In 1958, five Mauritanian leaders, including an Emir and former ministers, escaped to Morocco. Just as Togo sees no reason to cede its newly won independence to the larger and richer Ghana that seeks its association, so Mauritania does not wish to change rule by France for rule by Morocco. Since Mauritania was heavily dependent upon France for budgetary support after independence, her government was naturally conservative, pro-French, and anti-Moroccan. It is difficult to judge how many Mauritanians really wish to be ruled by Morocco, but they are only known to be considerable in Atar and some other northern oases. Morocco is not contiguous with Mauritania, from which she is separated by Algeria in the Tindouf area. This area Morocco claims on the same grounds; it also has rich resources of iron ore.

Morocco advanced across the Sahara and conquered the Songhay Empire in 1591, but its rule was not a good omen for the present day. Morocco, nevertheless, is friendly with Mali, which claims the relatively rich livestock country of Hodh in the southeast of Mauritania, and which was part of French Sudan (now Mali) until 1944.

For centuries Mauritanian nomads have lived from their cattle, camels, sheep, and goats. The blood, milk, and meat of these animals give food; their hides and skins provide materials for tents, saddles, water carriers, cushions, and mats; and their hair is used for brushes. Other than for subsistence, livestock are capital and status symbols, more than commercial stock, although sales are considerable to Senegal and the Gambia, and will increase. Camels are normally sold to Moroccan dealers, but political tension has stopped these sales.

The only other significant economic activity prior to 1960 was off-shore fishing by Canary Islanders and Europeans, and the air-drying of some of these catches in Port Etienne.

Arid Mauritania was so poor that under the French its capital was at St. Louis, Senegal. With autonomy, however, a capital had to be found within the country. A central point with water and reasonable communications was desirable, away from Moroccan influence and tribal jealousy. Nouakchott was designated in 1957; it lies 200 miles north-northeast of St. Louis in dry Sahel steppe, some 4 miles from a surfbound beach, on Mauritania's only north-south road, and has an excellent runway. Nevertheless, the site is one of flat loose sand, and water has to be brought 42 miles. The cost of this French gift of a new capital is some $8 million.

Nouakchott is the symbol of the new Mauritania that will find its viability through the opening up of rich iron-ore deposits in the Kedia d'Idjil Hills of the northwest, where there is very pure haematite ore averaging 63 per cent iron. At least 125 million tons can be worked open cast, as much underground, and there is additional poorer ore. The Miferma Company with French, British, German, and Italian capital, and a $66 million loan from the International Bank, is mining the deposit.

To reach the coast, a 400-mile railroad has been built from Fort Gouraud to Port Etienne, keeping outside Spanish Sahara because of onerous terms demanded by the Spanish for crossing their barren wastes. To avoid crossing the boundary at the southeastern corner, a 1.25 mile tunnel had to be built at a cost of $8.5 million, although an 8-mile crossing of Spanish Sahara would have avoided this. West of the tunnel, two belts of stabilized dunes are crossed, whereas at the head of the Cape Blanc peninsula active dunes may necessitate periodic realignment. Water, discovered on the railroad route 75 miles from Port Etienne, is carried into the town more cheaply than fresh water produced from Port Etienne's sea-water distillation plant.

The railroad ends in a new terminal with natural depths of 44 feet, permitting use by 65,000-ton ore carriers, which would have been impossible at Villa Cisneros (Spanish Sahara), the nearest port to the iron ore. Port Etienne is destined to become one of the world's great iron-ore shippers. It may also develop a meat- and fish-freezing plant and, possibly, become Mauritania's general port, saving her from long hauls via Dakar (Senegal). Port Etienne already receives intercontinental planes and some ten local flights per week.

By 1969, the Mauritanian government will be receiving $8.5 million per annum in royalties, which should permit it to balance the budget and free Mauritania from heavy dependence upon France. New townships at Tazadit (the mining headquarters), Port Etienne, and the new capital of Nouakchott will be symbols of the developing economy and state.

Mining of iron ore near Fort Gouraud may lead, through the relative proximity of the railroad, to opening other reserves south of Atar, and copper reserves with associated gold at Akjoujt, whereas petroleum is being prospected in western Mauritania as it is in Spanish Sahara.

Although on a lesser scale, the transformation of Mauritania from dire poverty to modest viability is like that of Arab sheikdoms consequent upon oil exploitation. Power politics are likewise involved; France needs a friendly Mauritania as a buffer between Morocco and Mali, radicals both cold toward France. She also needs Mauri-

tanian friendship on the Algerian western flank. Yet Mauritania and
the Algerians have the common bond of Islam. And could Mauritania survive if Morocco were given Spanish Sahara, which she also
claims?

MALI—LAND OF THE MIDDLE NIGER

Mali is the modern successor of ancient Mali, which, like Ghana
and Songhay, also had part of their realms here. Like the Niger
Republic, it is a large landlocked state, 600 miles from the nearest
port, Conakry in Guinea, separated from Mali by the high Fouta
Djallon. Although ancient Ghana, Mali, and Songhay benefitted
from their position on north-south routes, the virtual ending of
trade across the Sahara in modern times has put countries like
Mali and Niger at a severe disadvantage compared with the coastal
countries. Already better endowed with resources and nearer to
overseas trade routes, coastal lands further benefit from the transit
trade of the poorer inland countries.

Fully half the country, or an area larger than France, is too arid
for cropping of any kind. Parts of it are seasonally visited by
nomadic pastoralists who, nevertheless, must reckon on the seasonally inundated banks of the river Niger for the main feed of their
livestock. This livestock, fed, like other Tropical African livestock,
only on what they can find, are a major resource in Mali. Many are
driven south for slaughter, especially to Ghana but also to the
Ivory Coast.

The river Niger is an asset to Mali in many other ways. Rice is
being increasingly grown along its banks and in annually flooded
areas, as a result of better water control. The abandoned arms of
its former Inland Delta have been refilled with water from the
impressive barrage of the *Office du Niger,* completed in 1947 near
Sansanding. About 100,000 acres have been irrigated, mostly for
the cultivation of rice, but also for cotton, produced by some 27,000
Africans, resettled from poor areas of Mali and the Upper Volta.
The river is also the source of fish; some 30,000 tons of dried fish
being sold annually, even as far away as Ghana. The river is navi-

gable from Koulikoro (below the capital of Bamako) to Ansongo, although the weekly river service ends at Gao.

Peanuts are Mali's main cash export, and these are mostly grown in the west near the river, roads, and railway—the all-important lines of transportation.

The population of over 4 million is far larger than that of either Mauritania or the Niger, yet the local resources are still so mediocre that there is much periodic migration to the coastal lands for work.

Following the breakup of the Mali Federation in August, 1960, and the severance of relations with the former partner, Senegal, there were many fundamental economic and political changes. The hitherto vital Dakar-Niger Railway, which annually carried some 100,000 tons of Mali goods, was severed at the boundary, and other external links had to be developed. Houphouët-Boigny, President of the Ivory Coast (who needed to make a successful move at the same moment of the independence of his own country and of the other three members of the Benin-Sahel Entente), offered every help in developing the route from Bamako by road, and thence by rail to Abidjan, the Ivory Coast capital and excellent port. This not only gained more transit trade for the Ivory Coast, but saved Modibo Keita, the Mali President, from being entirely dependent upon Sekou Touré, the radical president of Guinea, who may feel jealous at the better treatment equally-radical Mali received from France in 1960, compared with what was given his country in 1958.

Nevertheless, in November, and December, 1960, Mali was glad to join the Ghana-Guinea Union, and the Union of African States came formally into being on July 1, 1961, with, however, few practical consequences. Mali would like to use the Guinea Railway and Kankan-Bamako road or Niger waterways, together the shortest route of all to the sea, but the railway is in poor repair and has a very low capacity.

The Mali Premier, perhaps more than most new African leaders, hopes for help from both West and East. For this, his central situation contiguous with Algeria and three members of the Benin-Sahel Entente, plus his membership of the contrasted Union of African

States, puts him in an excellent position. Of the three ex-French countries of West Africa that have common boundaries with Algeria, Mali has the longest and is the most outspokenly favorable to the Algerians. France had to evacuate her considerable bases in Mali.

Yet France has still thought it worthwhile to continue massive help to Mali, where she has spent over $100 million since World War II. Mali has also received token help from Britain and the United States.

Help promised from the East, however, is far greater. The Soviet Union has given a 12-year credit of $45 million at low interest to extend the Guinea Railway to Bamako and to prospect for and, if thought worthwhile, develop oil, gold, diamond and bituminous-shale mining. Navigation on the Niger will also be improved by removal of sandbanks, help will be given with the establishment of a cement works, and trade developed between the two countries. An economic and technical agreement was also signed in 1961 with China. Czechoslovakia is to help build textile and peanut oil mills, and a shoe factory. President Keita has said that there was no point in letting industry be financed by countries that would ultimately feel themselves threatened. The agreements are also in line with Keita's policy for a socialist society: "nationalism of all essential production, cooperative organization of all other sectors, and de-colonization of the economy to give Mali free choice in invest-ments." [2]

THE UPPER VOLTA—FRONTIER LAND OF THE BENIN-SAHEL ENTENTE
AND THE GHANA-GUINEA-MALI UNION

Although far smaller than the other dry lands of West Africa, the Upper Volta, nevertheless, is slightly larger than Colorado, or a little smaller than Italy. Its dry (although never desert) and poor environment has an unduly large population of over four million,

[2] President Modibo Keita, as reported in *West Africa* (London), August 26, 1961, p.944.

more than any other state of former French West Africa, except Mali.

The most famous of its peoples are the Mossi, whose kings date back to the early eleventh century. Ouagadougou was their capital from the fifteenth century, and it is the capital of the present republic. Although often surrounded by Islamic peoples, the Mossi never became converted. The frontier aspect of this country was thus evident at an early date.

This situation was re-emphasized under French rule: It was a separate colony from 1919 to 1932, but it was then parcelled out among its neighbors—the Ivory Coast, French Sudan, and Niger— to save administrative expense. It again became a separate territory in 1948 to limit the influence of the radical *Rassemblement Démocratique Africain,* then strong throughout the Ivory Coast but influential in what then became the Upper Volta only among the Bobo (area around Bobo Dioulasso, the second largest town), traditional rivals of the Mossi.

Division of interest was again evident early in 1959 when the country at first decided to join the Mali Federation, only to drop the idea later in the year at the behest of the Ivory Coast, with which it then became associated in the Benin-Sahel Entente. Nevertheless, the constitutional referendum showed that western Upper Volta had favored joining the Mali Federation.

Economically, the Upper Volta has long been closely associated with both the Ivory Coast and Ghana, in which at least 150,000 men are always working. Upper Volta overseas trade also passes through them, the dominant route being through Ghana until 1954, when the extension of the Abidjan-Bobo Dioulasso railroad reached Ouagadougou, and more trade was diverted down that line through the Ivory Coast. Yet there is little to sell, except poor livestock, peanuts, a little shea butter, and cotton, because the dry and poor soils barely support the large population. Water shortage is very acute, and diseases are widespread.

However, the Upper Volta also lies on an important trade route for Mali cattle and dried fish destined for Ghana; whereas in the other direction many goods are received from Ghana, officially and more so unofficially, because of the more varied sources of supply open to Ghana compared with the Ivory Coast, and the cheaper costs of transportation. (See Figure 6.) Thus, there have long been close economic ties with Mali and Ghana, as well as with the Ivory Coast. In 1961, the President of Upper Volta and Ghana agreed to abolish customs barriers between their countries. This should help local trade, especially Ghana importers and small dealers in the Upper Volta; the large importers will still be constrained by the tight controls of the Franc Zone to trade via the Ivory Coast. A little earlier the Upper Volta President refused to sign the Benin-Sahel Entente's jointly negotiated defense agreements with France.

The Upper Volta is thus the most hesitant and divided member of the Benin-Sahel Entente, and might easily join the Ghana-Guinea-Mali Union, with which its links are strengthening. It has the best of both worlds politically and is sought by both. Economically, however, it is landlocked and the poorest state in West Africa, with no immediate prospect of much development.

NIGER—THE DESERT FRINGE

The Niger Republic has an odd name, for the river Niger is far less important to or typical of it than is the case with Nigeria or Mali. Indeed, only a short and little-used reach of the river lies within the country, and that in its southwestern extremity.

Niger is the most politically and geographically landlocked of all West African countries. The Niger river cannot be used to and from the sea because of the Bussa rapids in Nigeria, and from Niamey, the capital, to the nearest port is 650 miles. Politically, nine-tenths of the Niger is also shut off from the sea by Nigeria, across which are the shortest routes to the sea for such towns of the southeast as Maradi and Zinder, the main commercial centers; but these routes are some 880 miles long and require relatively hard Nigerian Sterling for the transit. (See Figure 2.)

Larger than Mauritania but smaller than Mali, Niger extends 1,000 miles from southwest to northeast and 650 miles from north to south. One quarter of the country—the southern fringes—alone has more than 15 inches annual rain, whereas another quarter has 5 to 15 inches. One half has under 5 inches. (The annual average for Arizona is 7 inches.)

The quarter with over 15 inches is alone capable, in favored patches, of growing millet and other poor grains for food, with rice in seasonally flooded areas along the Niger river, and peanuts for food and sale (about 100,000 tons per annum). Suitable areas are mostly south of Maradi and Zinder, toward the Nigerian boundary, and in the southwest along the Niger river.

The quarter with between 5 and 15 inches of rain per year is the area of nomadic livestock and their Fulani or Tuareg herdsmen. These livestock, after peanuts, are the other main resource of the country. Large numbers are driven into Nigeria which offers a good market for their meat, hides, and skins. Goat skins are in demand abroad for glacé kid leather.

One half is more or less desert, with occasional seasonal pastures capable of supporting a few animals for a day or two a year, and with rare oases with brackish water. The east-central portion is pure desert with only one significant village—Bilma.

Niger is the only ex-French West African state still aided by the O.C.R.S. (Common Organization for the Saharan Regions), which is politically suspect to the other states. A convention signed in 1959 provides for help in five-sixths of the area of the country, particularly with well development.

In the north-central portion, however, the Aïr Massif is within the 5 to 15 inches rainfall zone, and from it flow numerous underground watercourses that may be tapped. Agadès is its center, a famous point on an old trans-Saharan route of which Zinder was the southern terminal. Agadès is a French air base for the defense of Algerian oilfields.

Niger was long a frontier land between the Songhay, Sokoto,

Tuareg, and Bornu Kingdoms. It is still a borderland between West Africa, the Sahara, North, and Central Africa (Chad). Naturally very poor, it was also at the end of French West African lines of communication.

Like Mauritania, Niger has no dominant core area, but rather three nodal areas that have divisive effects upon the country as a whole, and make any sort of national consciousness difficult to foster. The Tuareg of the Aïr Massif in the north center number some 250,000, were well organized until 1870, and revolted against the French during World War I. Very different are the 544,000 Djerma and Songhay of the southwest Niger valley lands centering on Niamey, the capital. Much separated from them are the 1,125,000 Hausa of the south-central Maradi-Zinder lands (Figure 5) who are separated by the boundary from the far more numerous Hausa of Nigeria. Their cultural and economic ties are with the south; and their allegiance to central government in Niamey, far away to the southwest, has sometimes wavered. Until 1926, Zinder, an old Hausa center as well as trans-Saharan caravan terminal, was the capital. This was then moved to Niamey to be less influenced by Nigeria in general, the Hausa in particular, and to be nearer the outer world.

To Hausa living on either side of the boundary and, in the past, governed very differently by France and Britain, important matters are: how much notice is respectively taken of their needs by the Niger Republic and by Nigeria, which offers the highest price for their peanuts, and the costs and routes of transportation. Peanut prices tend to be higher in the Niger Republic, but consumer goods are more expensive. The ideal is to sell nuts in Niger but to buy commodities in Nigeria, or to buy such articles that have been smuggled in from Nigeria. The situation is the same as between Senegal and the Gambia.

Since 1953 great encouragement has been given to the route through Niger by road to the Dahomey railhead at Parakou, and so to the roadstead of Cotonou. More than $6 million has been spent on improving this route, especially on the river Niger bridge. This route is the main economic link of these members of the Benin-Sahel Entente.

To move as many goods as possible by this route, the *Operation Hirondelle* compels traders to send certain goods, notably peanuts, by this long all-Franc route for some four months of the main trading season. The charge is only a little more than that of the far shorter and more efficient route through Nigeria, but foreign exchange is saved, local people are employed, and the Niger government pays the extra cost out of the additional revenue it gets.

Nevertheless, the Niger consumer necessarily pays more for his official imports, which for nine months per year must come in by the all-Franc route, whereas two-thirds of the peanuts and all the peanut oil still goes out through Nigeria, although the new deep water port at Cotonou, Dahomey, may reduce this partial dependence upon Nigeria. This was seen when, after France exploded nuclear devices in the Sahara, and Nigeria banned French ships and planes, Dahomey and Niger imports via Lagos were so disrupted that those countries soon begged Nigeria to lift the ban.

The economy of the Niger is exceedingly frail. There is little hope of mineral development, such as may transform Mauritania, or of playing off West and East which may help the less poor Mali, the moderately well-provided Guinea, and the relatively rich Ghana. Niger is very dependent upon France for aid, and upon Nigeria for transit of part of her overseas trade.

These mainly arid lands have been shut off from much contact with the world since the decline of trans-Saharan trade. Mauritania has iron ore, the quarrying of which will reduce her grim poverty, mainly nomadic life, and excessive dependence upon France. Mali and Niger seem to have no comparable resource with which to raise their standard of living, and must apparently seek development in improved transportation to offset their landlocked character. Mali's membership of the Union of African States and Niger's membership of the Benin-Sahel Entente, however, will enable them to enjoy the advantages and help of larger units.

B. LANDS OF TRANSITION AND EARLY
EUROPEAN CONTACT

SENEGAL—LAND OF NEGRO CULTURE

Senegal is a lowland country the size of Minnesota, or of England, Wales, and Scotland combined. It is the most westerly country of Africa, and also the most purely tropical one nearest to Europe. This position encouraged long and close contact with the latter, especially France, and caused it to be strongly influenced by European culture. Senegal was, in fact, France's oldest African colony.

The earliest contact was through the islets of Gorée (2 miles off modern Dakar) and St. Louis in the estuary of the Senegal river. These islets were French from 1659, although they consistently changed hands in wars with the Dutch and British. All Africans born on these islets, Rufisque and Dakar on the mainland, were, from 1916, automatically French citizens. These two islets and the other communes are not only the core areas of Senegal, but also of the former Federation of French West Africa.

The easiest entry into Africa was up the few navigable rivers. The best one in western West Africa was the Gambia, but it was controlled by the English from the sixteenth century. So the French used the alternative but inferior Senegal river, inferior because of its treacherous estuary and seasonal variation in flow, and therefore depth. The route up the Senegal river and down the Niger became the French trunk route of penetration into West Africa, but had the French possessed the Gambia river they would almost certainly have established a base well up that river and then proceeded inland. The Senegal river and the town of St. Louis would then have been of quite minor importance, "Dakar" might have developed up the Gambia river, and a shorter railroad built from there to the Niger. A fine river has been ruined by man by becoming divorced from its hinterland, the rational economic development of Senegal, almost divided into two limbs, was made most difficult (see GAMBIA).

Thus, St. Louis, in the Senegal river estuary, had at first to serve as a base. It was wholly natural, therefore, that educational and hospital facilities should have been earliest and most developed here, just as they were at Freetown (Sierra Leone), for long the headquarters of British West Africa. And just as from Freetown where the more educated descendants of freed slaves often found employment in the early Gold Coast, Nigeria, and elsewhere, so the more educated *Sénégalais* were found elsewhere in French West and Equatorial Africa, even to a great extent in far-off Gabon. Moreover, the word *Sénégalais* was used, and sometimes still is, to mean former "French West African," for example, *les Tirailleurs* Sénégalais in the French Army.

Senegal, unlike Sierra Leone, has retained its educational lead. It has some outstanding high or grammar schools attended by French children as well as African, the headquarters of the Institut Français d'Afrique Noire, and ex-French Africa's first university—Dakar. Such eminent men as Léopold Senghor, Senegal's President, philosopher, and poet; Mamadou Dia, its first Prime Minister and well-known economist; and Lamine Gueye, Mayor of Dakar, are eminent representatives of all that is best in Franco-African culture. Senghor has made a particular study of what he calls the symbiosis and dialogue between European and African cultures, and of African culture or *Négritude*.

The difficulties and dangers of the Senegal estuary, and the need for a calling point for boats on the South American service, prompted the construction of piers at Dakar, opposite Gorée, in the 1860's. They were so successful that the advantages of Dakar over St. Louis became evident immediately. It was decided to build West Africa's first railway from the river bank opposite St. Louis islet, 162 miles to Dakar, and to develop this as a port, therefore avoiding the Senegal estuary. The railway was opened in 1885, and thereafter Dakar also served as an outport for the Senegal valley. A through railway from Dakar to the Niger river was opened in 1924, which bypassed St. Louis and the Senegal valley route. However, St.

Louis remained a cultural center and the Senegal capital until 1958, when the capital was transferred to Dakar.

The fact that a superb port could be constructed in the shelter of the hook-like Cape Verde peninsula has facilitated the refuelling of much shipping on routes around Africa, between Europe and South America, and between West Africa and North America. Dakar now follows Le Havre and Marseilles in annually cleared commercial tonnage. Dakar is still a major naval, air, and military base.

During the life of French West Africa from 1904 to 1959, Dakar was the federal capital. As such, it had numerous government and commercial offices to serve an area three-fifths that of the United States. French bureaucracy employed large numbers of African and European civil servants, and their expenditure was a major element in local commerce.

In World War II the fine Yoff airport was built by American forces, and this free gift is supremely well placed for civilian air traffic on the same routes as shipping. After the war many industries were set up in and near Dakar, in the expectation that their market would be at least the whole of French West Africa.

Lastly, over a fifth of all French aid-expenditure in West Africa between 1947 and 1957 went to Dakar institutions and installations. It is not surprising that the other countries of the federation resented this, and reacted against it by refusing to come into a reformed federation with Senegal, except for the Sudanese Republic which stayed in only a year.

Dakar is now merely the capital of Senegal, which has only 5 per cent of the area and 12 per cent of the population of the old federation. Dakar industries no longer enjoy their former markets, and the port has lost the Mali transit trade since that country severed the railway link and developed transit through the Ivory Coast. Furthermore, there is the prospect of losing the Mauritanian transit trade, just as Mauritania is developing fast.

Yet Dakar has remained surprisingly prosperous. This is because western Senegal produces approximately 800,000 tons of peanuts annually, all by African farmers who also grow millet for food. The peanuts are almost all shelled and crushed locally for oil, which has a guaranteed market and high price in France, to enable it to complete, so the French say, with the United States price-supported soya bean. Peanut crushing was, in fact, Dakar's first large-scale industry.

Until recently, peanut products comprised over 95 per cent by value of Senegal exports; even now they account for about 85 per cent. But Senegal has been diversifying its economy, and this has also saved Dakar from depression. Large deposits of aluminum and calcium phosphate have been opened northwest of Thiès. Exports are developing, and the product may also save the peanut soils, so desperately in need of fertilizer. Dakar has also been helped by the development of tuna fishing and canning.

An ambitious economic plan has been drawn up involving the expenditure of $378 million. It stresses transportation and agriculture, more than industry and commerce. Specific industrial objectives include a calcium phosphate refinery, an oil refinery for Dakar, a chemicals industry, diversification and expansion of the textile industry, and the establishment of dispersed small industries. A barrage may later be built across the Senegal river for the generation of hydro-electric power that could be distributed to the existing towns and would greatly encourage industries, as well as regularizing the flow of the river and so improving its navigability. As at present defined, the boundary with Mauritania is along the Mauritanian bank, and thus the river is under Senegal control. Study of the river and its development is in the hands of the *Mission d'Aménagement du Sénégal* (M.A.S.), a body comparable in aims and function with the Tennessee Valley Authority.

East of the groundnut lands, the center of the country is almost empty and waterless. Only the northern arc of the Senegal valley, the western peanut lands, and the southern and better watered Casamance (south of the Gambia) are productive.

Senegal is cut into by the British virtual enclave of the Gambia; apart from the problems mentioned above, and in the section on the Gambia, it has greatly impeded equal attention to the development of the potentially significant Casamance. In 1959 this was at last linked by a direct road built (even in its Gambian portion) by the French. Gambia has been promised independence, but it could never be a viable state. Senghor has put it admirably: "the Gambians are, by nature and tribe, one with us. Their separateness is an accident of history. But they must first gain independence as a separate unit, with the boundaries they had in colonial times. After that, it is for them to choose."

Senegal is an outstanding example of an African country with three centuries of close European contact, of the development within a century of a peasant-grown crop of overwhelming importance nationally and internationally, and equally of a superb port. Advantages of geographical position have been grasped with striking results culturally and economically.

THE GAMBIA—"A FRANKFURTER INSERTED INTO A SENEGALESE ROLL"

Rights on the Gambia river, and later to James Islet 16 miles up river, were the first British possession in Africa, yet unlike other such footholds they never acquired a significant hinterland. The Gambia is now a 292-mile long riverine "wriggle" into the heart of Senegal, where the river, ceasing to be navigable all the year, becomes Senegalese. It is as if all the navigable Thames or Mississippi, together with narrow lands on either side, were held by another country.

The boundaries are straight lines and arcs of circles, dividing identical peoples on either side, but enclosing strips of land parallel to the navigable river, varying from 7 to 12 miles wide on each side. Between the river and the Senegal boundary to the north and the south there are usually no more than 2 or 3 villages. Thus, the boundary shuts off the excellent river from its otherwise extensive hinterland.

That more British territory was never obtained was due, in the first place, to a belief that the dry country to the north and east, and the wetter areas to the south were useless. Secondly, just when colonial expansion was taking place elsewhere, there were frequent Anglo-French discussions for the cession of the Gambia strip against French territory in the Ivory Coast, Dahomey, Guinea, Asia, or the Pacific. Interests in the Gambia, and misguided patriotism in Britain, prevented this early solution to a problem that historical neglect has grossly aggravated.

So the Gambia survived, to its own and Senegal's misfortune, and as a burden on Britain. Four times the size of Rhode Island, or of a medium-sized English county, its population is about 300,000. Political separation from its hinterland has meant that the river is used only by about 20 ocean-going ships a year, which come to carry overseas the mainly local peanut crop that constitutes over 95 per cent by value of the exports. Admittedly, many schooners concentrate the crop at two or three points for ocean vessels, but the Gambia Marine mail-carrying river boats, launches, and antique ferries frequently break down. One would have expected the river to be at least efficiently used by local boats, but limited revenues have made even this difficult. Roads, until recently two ruts through the thick bush and needlessly paralleling the river, were among the worst in Africa, and their use was prohibited for 5 months each year during the rains.

Separation from its hinterland has meant underemployment and poverty, although apparent content with a low standard of living and a touching devotion to Britain have been taken as indications that all was well. In consequence, the Gambia fell ever farther behind Senegal in political, social, and economic development.

One might also have supposed that every advantage would have been taken of this semi-enclave, but this has not been the case. Revenue-raising possibilites, such as regular international lotteries, plentiful issues of postage stamps, a free port, or the obvious peanut oil-extraction factories to attract peanuts from across the boundary, could have been considered.

The Gambia has been the scene of some ill-conceived plans for development. Three were failures by the Colonial Development Corporation; one was a fisheries project, another was a rice scheme that a river flood destroyed in its first year, and the third the notorious poultry scheme. This was directed by someone with no African experience; insufficient local feeding stuffs were available, and the scheme caused human food to rise steeply in price. The hen houses were so elaborate that they now serve as a teachers college! A private company started ilmenite mining only to run into a period of unfavorable prices. Thus, whereas Senegal, also overwhelmingly dependent upon peanuts, nevertheless, has furthered their processing and has the vast port of Dakar, phosphate mining, and tuna fishing, the Gambia has had no luck with diversification.

The Gambians are the impoverished orphans of an accident of colonial history—the political obstruction of the river. Their country has for long been unviable as a colonial unit, and it would plainly be so as an independent country, short of some most unlikely miracle such as striking oil—already prospected for but not found in commercial quantities.

Political integration or federation with Senegal would appear self-evidently desirable. There is a saying that every Gambian has a cousin in Senegal, and most have links across the boundary. The absurdity of the Gambia is evident on any map. Yet, separation has gone on for so long that the different colonial policies and methods of France and Britain have left uneffaceably different political, social, and economic imprints upon the two countries. Their official languages differ, as do their educational systems. Whereas Islam is strong in both, there is an overlay of Roman Catholicism in Senegal, and of the Church of England and Wesleyan Methodism in the Gambia. In Senegal there is a centralized administration in which chiefs have for decades played no part, but in the Gambia they have been sustained in power, although most are illiterate. In Senegal taxation is mostly indirect, particularly on consumer imports, and the cost of living is high. In the Gambia, taxation is more direct, imports are cheap and varied in origin, and the cost of living much lower. On the other hand, wheras high guaranteed prices are still accorded by France for Senegal peanuts and peanut oil, the Gambia gets a much lower price, more related to the world figure. Senegal is, of course, a member of the tightly organized Franc Zone, Gambia of the freer Sterling Bloc.

Association, federation, and still more so, complete integration with Senegal would thus be most difficult. Not surprisingly, the Gambian chiefs are against it, for they would lose their power; whereas the Bathurst civil servants and commercial people fear they would be unemployed. Many Gambian imports are really destined for smuggling over the border. The cost of living in the Gambia would undoubtedly rise, and the variety of goods decline. It is uncertain whether France would wish to pay high prices for even more peanuts and peanut oil than she can absorb even now. The Senegalese railway fears competition from cheaper river navigation on the parallel river Gambia, the more so since the railway suffered from the severed link with Mali. Although Bathurst would be much better off if river traffic developed, it would be in a much worse condition if it did not, and certainly so in competition with the mighty and efficient Dakar with its fine port, airport, and industries. Bathurst would cease to be a capital, and its nascent oil extraction industry would face great uncertainty at the very least. Meanwhile, technical cooperation is developing in such matters as transportation, telecommunications, and agriculture through a permanent committee.

The Gambia, a deep colonial semi-enclave in an independent country, is fortunate in its patient neighbor, with its belief that the future of the Gambia is a matter for the Gambians. The difficulties and costs of incorporation are well understood, and there may be time to see how the Somali and Cameroon republics succeed, both of which incorporate two territories brought up in contrasted ways by their former rulers.

Those countries might provide direct lessons to a new Senegambia, an historical name from the short-lived British colony of 1765-1783 resulting from conquest of Gorée and St. Louis. It remains difficult to know how to develop a ministerial system if the Gambia may later lose it, and how to prepare for sovereign status that may later be transferred. Yet, a successful Senegambia could be a third example in West Africa of integration across old colonial boundaries, of which the Ghana-Guinea-Mali Union was the first, and the Cameroon Federation the second.

C. LAST FOOTHOLDS OF ANCIENT COLONIALISM

THE PORTUGUESE OVERSEAS PROVINCES OF CAPE VERDE,
GUINEA, SÃO TOMÉ, PRÍNCIPE, AND THE SPANISH
OVERSEAS PROVINCE OF FERNANDO PO.

The ten volcanic islands and five islets of the Cape Verde group are half as large again as Rhode Island, or less than one-third the size of Northern Ireland. Lowland Portuguese Guinea is about the size of Massachusetts and Connecticut combined, or half the size of Scotland. The third Portuguese overseas province in West Africa is São Tomé and Príncipe, two islands of volcanic origin six times the size of the District of Columbia, or a little over half as large again as the Isle of Man.

These relics of Portugal's early discoveries and of her vast interest in the slave trade hardly warrant much space here, or a disquisition on Portuguese policy,[3] but since Portugal presently has no intention of ever voluntarily relinquishing these provinces, despite the tide of independence around them, some mention should be made.

Portugal believes she has (and that the other ex-colonial powers ought to have had) a civilizing mission in Africa that she cannot relinquish. Furthermore, since these provinces are as much a part of Portugal as any metropolitan ones, she cannot surrender her own soil. That independence has come all around, only strengthens her belief in the immorality of the demand that she should grant it. The Portuguese counter twentieth-century arguments with those of the Crusades.

Needless to say, even if independence were theoretically envisaged, it would not be possible for tiny São Tomé and Príncipe; for the

[3] An excellent source is Duffy, James, *Portuguese Africa,* Cambridge, Mass., Harvard University Press, 1959.

Cape Verde Islands and Portuguese Guinea it could only come in some form of association or union with Senegal or Guinea, or division among them. Exiles have formed several liberation movements in Dakar and Conakry, and a United Liberation Front was formed in Dakar in 1961. In recent years there have been disturbances in São Tomé and Portuguese Guinea, and in 1961 some exiles entered Portuguese Guinea from Senegal and attacked buildings at Santo Domingo, just over the boundary. When these exiles were pursued into Senegal, that country broke off diplomatic relations. It is surprising that Senegal, rather than Guinea, should wish to "liberate" Portuguese Guinea; perhaps this is done so that Senegal will not be thought backward in attacking colonialism.

The Cape Verde Islands are fertile but very arid, over populated, and little developed; thus São Vicente, a fueling port, although well-sited, is much less frequented than Las Palmas (Grand Canary, Spanish), or Dakar, Senegal. Poverty has driven many Cape Verdians to work in other Portuguese provinces.

Portuguese Guinea is a country of rivers and estuaries, where some excellent rice cultivation is done in reclaimed swamps; and where groundnuts, grown in the drier interior, are the main export. These products, palm oil and kernels, and copra, account for 90 per cent of the exports, and are sent mainly to Portugal and handled by a company whose works is the largest industrial unit in Lisbon.

São Tomé and Príncipe are rich and precipitous volcanic islands that are well watered because of their equatorial situation. There are large company or absentee landlord-owned plantations, one of which occupies 25,000 acres, one-tenth of São Tomé. Cocoa is by far the main crop, and until 1905 these islands were the leading world exporters. After 1908 British chocolate firms ceased purchases after revelations of slave-like conditions on the plantations. Forced labor is still used, despite which the United States purchases one-third of the crop.

The Spanish have the same views of their African footholds as the Portuguese, and the province of Fernando Po (Fernando Po island, 784 square miles, and Annobon, 7) is similar in physical character, and social and economic conditions to São Tomé and Príncipe, save that labor (some 20,000 men) is fully paid and comes mainly from Eastern Nigeria to work on the otherwise similar cocoa estates. These highly politically conscious Ibo from independent Nigeria might introduce nationalistic ideas to the island.

It seems certain that Portuguese Guinea—the only mainland territory—will ultimately be incorporated in an independent state or states, but the islands may remain as relics of European rule.

D. LANDS OF THE SOUTHWEST COAST

GUINEA—LAND OF VARIETY AND POLITICS

Guinea, which is one-eighth larger than the United Kingdom, and about the size of Colorado but with twice its population, is an extremely varied country of great interest and potential.

Its marshy coast, with many mangrove-studded estuaries, has only two ridges reaching the sea—one at Cape Varga and the other at Conakry. The latter was developed because a route was possible from it into the interior.

Behind the coast is a lowland plain on which rice, the main food crop of the country, is grown extensively. The oil palm is also significant, although much less so than in the past or in present-day neighboring Sierra Leone. The area is farmed by Soussou and other peoples who were pushed into the area from the Niger valley several centuries ago. Recent development has centered first on banana cultivation started by Europeans and Lebanese, and, since 1950, on bauxite and iron ore mining. The former is on Kassa, one of the Los Islands off Conakry with prospective developments at Boké near the northern end of the coast. Lateritic iron ore is worked opencast eight miles inland from Conakry. (See Figure 4.)

Inland rises the often impressive fault scarp of the Fouta Djallon, a level tableland divided by deeply trenched rivers with tortuous courses. Through valley routes are few, and valleys and plateaus seldom meet. The latter are poor, level, and often lateritic seasonal pasture lands used by the Fulani, while the valleys sometimes

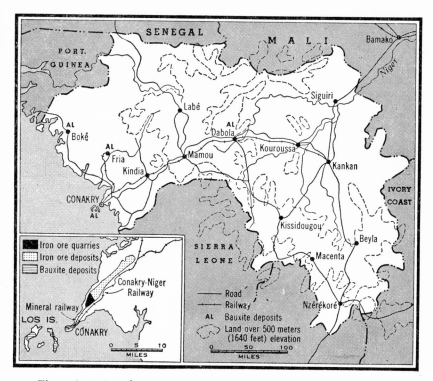

Figure 4   Guinea (Based on maps in R. J. Harrison Church, *West Africa*)

have citrus and pineapple groves on their slopes, with bananas in the valley floors, again started by expatriates with local Malinke labor.

Hydroelectric power potential is considerable in the Fouta Djallon, despite the seasonal character of rainfall and rivers. Its development has been mainly proposed by means of a dam and power station on the Konkouré river, which would provide power to make aluminum. Meanwhile, alumina is produced at Fria from local bauxite.

To the east are the poor and likewise often laterized plains of the Upper Niger and its tributaries, where rice is grown in water-controlled areas near the rivers, and drier cereal crops grown away from them.

In the Guinea Highland foothills, diamonds are worked open-cast north and east of Macenta. To the south rise the impressive forest clad Guinea Highlands, frontier lands of Guinea and Liberia. As also in the latter, these mountains have rich reserves of iron ore, and have been planted extensively with coffee, a crop that accounts for one-third of Guinea's exports by value. Again, this crop is grown on plantations originally owned by expatriates.

Guinea probably has the richest potential of all the former members of French West Africa; it is certainly far more diversified in its agricultural and mineral production than any other member. Yet Guinea has been severely affected by soil erosion, by vast plateau surfaces of laterite, and difficult and thus costly means of transportation. The Conakry-Kankan railroad was built by the French in the first years of the century in the face of formidable physical and, indeed, other difficulties, and much of the track resembles a Swiss or Rocky-Mountain line.

The river Niger, and especially its tributary the Milo, are navigable respectively from Kouroussa and Kankan downstream to Bamako, the Mali capital. But rapids prevent further direct carriage and, in any case, this navigation is more potentially significant to Mali as a route for external trade than to Guinea. The same is truer of the parallel roads.

A good road links N'Zérékoré and the Guinea Highland area generally with the Liberian free port of Monrovia, but traffic is not considerable since the withdrawal of French technicians, because of frequent congestion in Monrovia port and the coolness of Guinea-Liberia relations. On the other hand, the port of Conakry is well-equipped to handle bananas, iron ore, and alumina brought to the port by the Conakry-Niger railroad and two mineral lines.

Guinea, like Pakistan, is very much the result of the attitude of one man. Sekou Touré, who has long been a radical, directed his people to say "No" to de Gaulle's Referendum on 28 September, 1958. Guinea was cast adrift four days later, French administrators (three-quarters of the total in Guinea) and technicians were withdrawn, and all movable French property taken away. Although

France had to reward the loyalty of the other members of the then French West Africa, she need not have been so deliberately harsh or shortsighted. Nor need have France's allies. Guinea was forced to seek aid from anyone offering it, and Ghana was one of the first. A loan of $28 million was offered, and the Ghana-Guinea Union came into existence in December, 1958.

It was a golden opportunity for the Communist countries, yet Guinea has remained anxious for trade and contacts with all countries. Communist and Capitalist systems are both evident in economic life, and cooperatives have become important. A new Franc was created in 1960 and trade, which until then had still been largely with the French Franc Zone, has declined considerably with it. Coffee, bananas, and palm kernels, once largely exported to France and Algeria, are now sold mainly to Eastern Europe. Other exports to Eastern Europe are likely to increase, as are imports from there. Many development projects have also been undertaken, notably the rebuilding by Russia of the Conakry-Kankan railroad and its possible extension into Mali to Bamako. China has also provided ill-spared rice, a loan, and buildings.

Yet enterprises from non-Communist countries have been welcomed, and nine Japanese steel companies, in association with West European capital, decided in late 1961 to develop rich iron ore deposits on the Guinea side of Mount Nimba and Mount Simandou. Similarly, Guinea's largest development, the Fria bauxite and alumina plant, 96 miles north-northeast of Conakry, is owned by an international group comprising Olin Mathieson Chemical Corporation (United States—48.5 per cent), Péchiney and Ugine metallurgical and chemical concerns (French—26.5 per cent), British Aluminium Company Ltd. (10 per cent), Aluminium-Industrie A.G. (Swiss—10 per cent), and Vereinigte Aluminiumwerke A.G. (German—5 per cent). This development had an initial capacity to produce 480,000 metric tons of alumina from local bauxite reserves estimated at 200 million tons. The plant may later produce 1,440,000 tons annually, making it the world's largest producer. Alumina was first shipped in 1960 to Canada, Europe, and Cameroon; it was shipped to Cameroon for manufacture into aluminum at the Edea smelter by the hydro-electric power station and barrage on the Sanaga river.

The Fria alumina works in Guinea is one of the largest and most modern in the world, and some 2,000 workers are employed—one half of all Guinea's paid labor in 1960. Sabende township, with 5,000 inhabitants, was specially constructed, as was a railroad to Conakry, a new quay, and storage facilities for oil and alumina. Up to 1960, $150 million had been invested, but the Souapiti earth dam (25 miles away on the Konkouré river), a power station, and aluminum works —all essential to the long-term viability of Fria—were not built. This was mainly because of political uncertainty following Guinea's independence, but partly because of temporary excess capacity in world aluminum production. Construction of the dam has been discussed with both West and East. If the latter carried out the final works, then the earlier sections would most likely be nationalized.

The development of the Boké bauxite deposits, with reserves of 700 million tons, has been more checkered. It was started in 1958 (for completion by 1964) by Bauxites du Midi, Aluminium Limited of Canada's French subsidiary, but was later joined by Reynolds Aluminum and Kaiser Aluminum from the United States, and Péchiney and Vereinigte Aluminiumwerke A.G. to provide vital extra capital. The last two firms were thus in both the Fria and Boké schemes in a relatively minor way. The project, one-sixth more costly than the Fria one, likewise provided for alumina and aluminum factories (output of 220,000 tons annually of metal), a railroad, and harbor at Boké. The last two had been partly completed, when, in the Fall of 1961, Aluminum Ltd. suspended further development owing to financial difficulties. Further capital was needed which, in view of political uncertainties in Guinea, it was felt unfair to ask of shareholders, and the United States Government had been unwilling to help. Again, the extra capacity was not needed in 1961-62, and there were possibilities that direct manufacture of aluminum from bauxite would make the plant obsolete upon completion. On the other hand, Guinea has large reserves of bauxite, and the West is not anxious to see Communist countries control these reserves, which are as relatively important to aluminum producers as Middle East Oil reserves are to petroleum refiners.

Suspension of further development was also politically embarrassing to President Sekou Touré, since it facilitated Communist pressure upon him. Indeed, Czech, Hungarian, Polish, and Soviet technicians soon arrived to take over exploitation of the Kassa (Los Islands) bauxite deposit, from which the same company had been exporting about 350,000 tons of bauxite annually, mostly to Canada, since 1953. Most is now going to Poland, but the deposit will soon be exhausted.

Suspension of development by the company led to a presidential decree ending the activities in Guinea of the Compagnie des Bauxites du Midi, but it was given the chance of reinstatement if the Boké project was soon restarted. The Guinea government emphasized that "industrialization means the transformation of primary products within the country, and not the perpetuation of the colonial method based on the extraction of minerals for shipment and processing abroad." Many would approve this sentiment, if local processing were economic; if not, one cannot expect any private company, foreign or otherwise, to engage in charity. In the end, the Boké concession was given to Harvey Aluminum of America in November, 1962.

Lateritic iron ore output rose steadily from its beginning in 1953, but in 1957 output fell back to less than in 1953. Britain (which provided one-third the capital) has always taken most, and Poland is now taking about a third. Reference has been made to far richer haematite iron ore located in the remote Mt. Nimba area.

Open-cast diamond mining dates from 1935, and the company concerned until 1961 was a member of the De Beers group. As in Sierra Leone, there were many illicit diggings, and part and then all the concessions were nationalized. Since the formation of cooperatives, illegal mining has declined, and a local purchasing center at Kankan has put an end to formerly extensive smuggling into Sierra Leone and Liberia.

Enough has been said to demonstrate the variety and significance of Guinea's resources. Their successful development now depends mainly on political considerations.

SIERRA LEONE—MOTHER OF FORMER BRITISH WEST AFRICA

Just as Senegal was the base from which former French West Africa largely developed, so Sierra Leone was the mother of most of former British West Africa. It is a small country, only a little larger than Ireland or West Virginia. Moreover, its northeastern half is very mountainous, and much of the coast is swamp. However, its overseas trade is larger than that of either its larger neighbors, Guinea and Liberia, largely because of lucrative diamond production that is now mainly accomplished by African diggers.

Like Liberia, but antedating it, Sierra Leone originated in Freetown as a home for freed slaves who came here from Britain, as British refugees from the newborn United States, the West Indies, and from slave ships captured in West African waters. African soldiers, discharged after the Napoleonic Wars, were also settled in such appropriately named villages as Wellington and Waterloo, southeast of Freetown. A Crown Colony had been created in 1808 of the small area around Freetown.

There thus grew up an African settler community around the fringes of the high Sierra Leone peninsula, as different from the rest of the country as Gibraltar from Spain, or Hong Kong from China. These settlers were detribalized, often of mixed blood, non-African in culture, and with nothing in common and having no contact with indigenous Africans. The settlers became known as Creoles, akin to those in the West Indies, the Seychelles, the Comoro Islands, and Réunion. Their way of life is European or that of the Southern States of the United States. Thus, until recently, the dominant style of house architecture in Freetown, and especially in Liberian coastal towns, was American Colonial, with timber pillars supporting a balcony.

Education was especially cherished, and Fourah Bay College, Freetown, has been giving some form of university education since

1827, fully a century earlier than anywhere else in West Africa, and long before there was a Ministry of Education in the United Kingdom or the United States. Sierra Leoneans thus provided most of the early African professional classes and clerks in the then Gold Coast and Nigeria, which were also governed from Freetown for many years of the nineteenth century. Their work, inspiration, and sacrifice helped greatly in bringing those countries into close contact with western civilization. Here is an exact counterpart with educated Africans from Senegal and, later, Dahomey, found throughout former French West Africa. There, as in ex-British West Africa, other lands have since proved richer and more productive, and the Senegalese, Dahomeans, and Sierra Leoneans have found this difficult to accept.

The greatest rift, however, was in Sierra Leone itself. The bulk of the country, the former Protectorate, did not become part of Sierra Leone until just over a century after the arrival of the first freed slave African settlers. The two parts really only came together after World War II, and it was difficult for the Creoles of the Colony, Christian and educated as they were, and considering Britain as their home, to feel one with the indigenous Africans of the Protectorate. Constitutional progress and universal suffrage inevitably meant the end of the dominance of the 30,000 Creoles over some 2 million indigenous Africans. With universal suffrage, the majority party and the prime minister naturally came from the peoples of the Protectorate. Furthermore, almost all the productive resources of Sierra Leone were found there. Thus, the contrast lay between the educated minority of the Colony, and the less educated majority in the Protectorate, with its greater economic resources. With independence this rivalry and jealousy has diminished with the abolition of the old administrative divisions of Colony and Protectorate, but its effects are still noticeable in the small-town character of much that is Sierra Leonean.

Sir Milton Margai, prime minister before and after independence, is a distinguished doctor who did outstanding work in the Protectorate. He is very friendly to the West and with Nigeria, where many Sierra Leoneans still live and from where many students come to study at Fourah Bay College. It is also from Nigeria that many Freetown Creoles think most of their ancestors came.

With Liberia there are the close ties of a similar origin, but it should be remembered that while the Americo-Liberians, the descendants of freed slaves, are still mainly the governing body in Liberia, their counterpart, the Freetown Creoles, are not now dominant in the Sierra Leone Government. Furthermore, Liberia lost territory to Sierra Leone between the present boundary and the Sewa river in 1885. (See Figure 5.) Although this has never been the subject of any outward resentment by Liberia, it might become so in the future. Until 1961, the two countries had no direct road link, but a good one now joins them. There are several fair roads into Guinea, but differences of origin and present political outlook are such that relations are less close than with Liberia.

Like its two neighbors, Sierra Leone has been transformed by mineral developments. Mineral exports first surpassed agricultural ones in 1953; by 1960 mineral exports accounted for two-thirds of the total. This is mainly due to diamond mining, a country-wide monopoly in the hands of one company until 1956. For some four years before that time, extensive illegal digging and smuggling of diamonds over the borders into Liberia or Guinea lost the government so much revenue that the monopoly had to be ended. The company continues mining and accounts for about one-quarter of the total diamond production. In 1950 diamond exports were worth $3.92 million and in 1960 $46.2 million; Sierra Leone in 1960 was the world's fourth largest diamond producer. Diamonds now account for about one half of Sierra Leone's overseas trade, and iron ore, which has good prospects, accounts for most of the other minerals. Bauxite and rutile are being developed, but the production of chromite and gold has greatly declined. It is this growth in mineral—especially diamond—exports, and the licenses, royalties, taxation, and export duties paid, that have made independence economically supportable.

Palm kernels, the leading crop until 1953, are still the main agricultural one, but cocoa and coffee are becoming important. Rice is the main food crop, but some costly efforts have been made to grow greater quantities that might more economically be imported. Banana plantations are being developed; they could have been long ago if British banana boats had called in this area. Rubber plantations should also succeed in view of their success in similar conditions in Liberia.

Although nature lavished a fine deep estuary upon Sierra Leone at Freetown, the only such natural harbor in West Africa, no deep water quay was opened until 1953. The advantages of the estuary have, in fact, only been fully realized in wars, when convoys have gathered here in great numbers. This could long have been, and still could be, a fine site for a free port—a West African Aden, Hong Kong, or Curaçao. Such enterprise has not been much evident in the past in Sierra Leone; it is greatly needed now if such a small country and population, with a low per capita income and poor soils, is to prosper.

LIBERIA—"THE LOVE OF LIBERTY BROUGHT US HERE"

Like Sierra Leone, Liberia originated in the settlement of freed slaves, in this case by Americans. After an unsuccessful attempt to initiate a settlement on Sherbo Island, Sierra Leone, in 1820, a group was established by the American Colonization Society on Providence Islet, Monrovia, in 1822. Other groups were founded along the coast, by this and other societies. In 1847, most of these settlements proclaimed their independence as Liberia, and took as their national motto the words "The Love of Liberty Brought Us Here." The country was promptly recognized by the United Kingdom, but the issue of Slavery, then dividing the United States, delayed American recognition until the Civil War. In 1857 the colony of Maryland in Liberia, with its capital at Harper, was admitted as a county. By 1867, some 13,136 former slaves had crossed from America to Liberia, and 5,722 more had been put ashore by the United States Navy or other United States Government agencies, but after the end of the Civil War the flow practically ceased.

Liberia, a collection of scattered settlements along a fever-ridden and utterly inhospitable coastline, with about 130 inches of rainfall annually, poor soils, and a totally unknown hinterland of backward peoples, faced formidable problems.

As in Sierra Leone, the ex-slaves knew nothing of tribal life, were American rather than African, and did not consider themselves African. They lacked skills, capital, experience, or interest in their new environment. The American Colonization Society gave gifts but little or no technical training. Even if the ex-slaves had acquired such training, they were then more anxious to live as their former masters then did in the United States, than to work hard. They built houses in the style of Southern State homes; at best they considered the indigenous Africans as children or barbarians, and at worst as their slaves.

A 40-mile coastal strip was divided into 6 counties, and the rest was divided into provinces. Effective government barely extended over all coastal settlements, certainly not beyond the counties, and this situation prevailed until the years between World Wars I and II. There is thus a close parallel between the attitude of the Sierra Leone Creoles in their Colony, and the indigenous Africans of the Protectorate at the time.

Liberia is the sole country of Africa never to have been a colony of a European power. President Tubman is on record as saying that, in consequence, Liberia missed the good consequences of colonial rule—transportation facilities and technical help in developing agriculture, commerce, and industry. Even her mentor, the United States, gave her little practical help between 1847 and 1942, partly for fear of appearing colonialist. The indigenous Africans often attacked the settlers, the British took territory west of the Mano river in 1885, the French east of the Cavally river in 1892. (See Figure 5.) The latter was done to secure some of the Kru people, adept workers on ships. When the French proposed a boundary along the right bank of the river, the Liberian delegate hastened to agree, thinking, as a non-geographer and looking unknowingly at the map, that he would thus secure the river for Liberia. Only after the convention was signed did Liberia realize that France had the river. This has had some significance since the advent of the Firestone Company, as they have a small plantation on the Cavally river. To send their rubber down the river, permission had to be obtained from the Ivory Coast.

The miracle of Liberia is that she survived. She did so largely in isolation and on a subsistence basis until the advent of the Firestone Rubber Company in 1926. After some two years of discussion, the company secured a concession of up to a million acres. In return, a large loan was granted to the Liberian government, with the prospect of substantial royalties and taxes, the rates of which have since increased. Only about a quarter of the concession has been rented, and of that about a half has been planted with some 12 million trees, producing about 45,000 tons of rubber annually. This is by far the largest rubber operation in the world, with the greatest concentration of high yielding rubber trees. Yet, Liberian rubber provides only about one-third of Firestone's natural rubber requirements, and under one-sixth of its total needs of rubber. Firestone exports of rubber began in 1933, and developed rapidly after 1938. During the war Liberia and Ceylon were the Allies' only sources of natural rubber. In 1945, rubber exports, overwhelmingly from the Firestone estates, still accounted for 96.6 per cent of Liberian exports.

The early 1940's saw great changes. In 1942, America was given the right to station troops in Liberia, and while there they built Roberts Field airport, adjacent to Firestone's main estate and 55 miles from Monrovia. This was for some 15 years Liberia's only international airport. American forces also built a road through the center of the country from Monrovia to the Guinea border, now linked to N'Zérékoré in Guinea. This has been of great value in opening the center of Liberia, and by being a spine from which to project other roads west and east through the interior. It has also opened a short route to a port for southern Guinea, which is very remote from the Guinean port of Conakry. The greatest benefit Liberia received from America, however, was the deep-water harbor of Monrovia built between 1945 and 1948 at a cost of $20 million.

Like most other West African artificial harbors, it consists of long breakwaters (here 7,702 and 7,250 feet in length) built in the face of heavy surf to enclose a large space of calm deep water. This is West Africa's only free port.

President Tubman first took office in 1944 and he is a statesman of world stature, even though president of a state only the size of Indiana, or Scotland plus Northern Ireland. He brought needed energy and enlightenment into the government, even if he mixed it with some of the autocracy of the century-old one party rule of his True Whigs. From the developing Firestone estates, and the air, road, and port services, he has acquired revenue to develop more roads and start welfare services, both previously so deficient. He has especially granted numerous and varied concessions to companies of diverse nationalities, for example, for iron-ore mining (mainly American, Swedish, and German), banana cultivation (German), pharmaceutical supply (British), airline (German), telephones (Swedish), and hydro-electric power (Belgian).

Of these, iron-ore exploitation initiated a new era in Liberian economic history. The first concession, granted to an American company, brought forth Liberia's first railroad, opened in 1951, when iron-ore exports began; in 1961, when a second concession on the Mano river began operating, exports of iron looked likely to overtake those of rubber in value. A vast Liberian-Swedish-American enterprise is developing ore production on Mt. Nimba; from here it will be transported by Africa's first remote-controlled railroad to a specially built harbor at Buchanan (Grand Bassa). Other iron-ore concessions are being developed, and by 1970 Liberia may be one of the world's great iron-ore exporters. With Mauritania, Guinea, Sierra Leone, and Liberia, West Africa is becoming a major world area for iron ore.

Liberia still has many difficulties. Its concession type of production is, in its technique, more colonial than the economies of many colonies ever were. True, the royalties and taxes have always accrued to an independent government, but they provide only wage earning employment and occupy large areas of land, little of which can be used for food crops. There is almost none of the enthusiastic production by individual African farmers, so characteristic of most West African food and cash crops. Indeed, very few of Liberia's exports are produced by Liberians on their own land and by their own initiative.

The large number of concessions has raised another acute problem, that of labor. The population of Liberia is very small, much less than the commonly quoted 1.5 to 2.5 million. Liberia is the only West African country for which there is no reliable official estimate or census. Indeed, the government was for long averse to taking a census for fear of revealing a very low figure, and thus deterring concessionaires and also United Nations agencies from making per capita grants based on a much higher figure. Many concessions have experienced labor shortage, for example, the Bomi Hills iron ore mine and Firestone.

For long, communications were, perhaps, the most acute problem, but a bare framework is at last beginning to appear. President Tubman is also breaking down the old division between the Counties and Provinces, and has had several indigenous Africans in his government. Administration has become far more enlightened and efficient. Firestone, American aid, President Tubman, and iron ore have together brought vast changes to Liberia since 1926.

Lands of the southwest coast, which include Portuguese Guinea, are characterized by heavy monsoonal rainfall and heavily leached soils. Agriculture, therefore, is best carried on in coastal and inland swamps that are well-suited to rice cultivation, the main food crop. Guinea and Liberia have been much developed by plantation agriculture, the former mainly for coffee, bananas, citrus fruits, and pineapple, the latter for rubber; Sierra Leone is now starting banana plantations. Guinea, Sierra Leone, and Liberia have been, or are being, transformed by the development of minerals—mainly bauxite but also diamonds and iron in Guinea, mainly diamonds but also iron in Sierra Leone, and iron almost alone in Liberia. The area is becoming a major world exporter of iron.

Politically, the countries provide great contrasts—Portuguese Guinea, relic of another age; Guinea, dynamic and anxious for help from the West, yet politically happier in the Communist bloc; Sierra Leone and Liberia, ex-slave in origin, their existence due to British and American efforts at expiation for their part in the slave trade and slave keeping, strongly traditionalist and conservative in atmosphere, and nearer Portuguese Guinea than the Republic of Guinea.

E. LANDS OF THE SOUTHERN OR GUINEA COAST

THE IVORY COAST—ECONOMIC CORE OF FORMER FRENCH WEST AFRICA AND OF THE PRESENT BENIN-SAHEL ENTENTE

The Ivory Coast, one of the larger countries of the Guinea coast, is about the size of New Mexico, or of the United Kingdom with the Benelux countries. One-third larger than Ghana, it nevertheless has less than half the population of that neighbor. This was probably because the forest was denser in the Ivory Coast, its coast even more inhospitable, and its fragmented peoples did not develop such an advanced or large political unit as Ashanti.

Guaranteed high prices for coffee, cocoa, and bananas in France have brought prosperity to the country. As in Guinea, the French granted concessions for plantations to French and Lebanese citizens and companies, so that these crops, as in Guinea, are produced on plantations as well as by small African farmers, who in Ghana are alone responsible for cocoa production.

Development has especially been hastened by the opening in 1950 of the Vridi Canal across the sandspit separating the Ebrié Lagoon (on which stands Abidjan, the capital) from the sea. Abidjan thus became a fine, deep and completely sheltered seaport, an artificial analogue of the naturally open Lagos (Nigeria). This canal led to an enormous development of external commerce, further stimulation of agriculture, forestry, the beginnings of mining, as well as to a great expansion of the town of Abidjan and of industry in its island suburb of Treichville. Abidjan has a far richer hinterland than Dakar (Senegal) and is the headquarters of the Benin-Sahel Entente.

Some $50 million of French aid was spent on improvements in Abidjan from 1947-1957.

As in neighboring Liberia and in the richer Ghana, manpower is short. There has long been seasonal, periodic, and permanent immigration from the economically and politically associated Upper Volta, for which the Ivory Coast is also the door to the outside world via the Abidjan-Ouagadougou railroad.

In consequence, the Ivory Coast was the richest of the eight partners of former French West Africa. Its overseas trade represented nearly one-half that of the Federation, and Ivory Coast revenues contributed far more than it received. The country not unnaturally became the center of anti-federalism, of dislike of the old French West Africa—so highly centralized in far-off Dakar, developed out of federal revenues largely contributed by the richer Ivory Coast to the poorer Senegal. When the Federation of French West Africa was breaking up in 1958-59, and Senegal was seeking to renovate it in the new Mali Federation, the Ivory Coast premier, M. Houphouët-Boigny, led the opposition and helped to dissuade the Upper Volta and Dahomey from joining. As a counter to the Mali Federation, and to Ghana, he brought together in 1959, the Upper Volta, Dahomey, and its economically closely associated Niger, in the Benin-Sahel Entente.

M. Houphouët-Boigny, a staunch Francophile, ardently supported the French Community as first conceived in 1958-59 as a close association in which foreign affairs, defense, and much more would be jointly agreed by France and her partners. When, however, the Mali Federation of Senegal and the Sudanese Republic was in December, 1959, promised full independence (after working out the details of agreements with France), M. Houphouët-Boigny felt let down by President de Gaulle. To retain his following, he was soon constrained to claim immediate independence for the members of the Benin-Sahel Entente before they signed any agreements with France. Those four countries thus left the Community and became fully independent in 1960.

When the Mali Federation collapsed in August, 1960, and the

Mali Republic (formerly the Sudanese Republic and French Sudan) refused to let its overseas trade continue to pass through Senegal, it was encouraged to use the road-rail route to Abidjan. That port is thus the trade door for Mali, the Upper Volta, and the Ivory Coast, and the latter seems destined to be the economic center of ex-French West Africa.

GHANA—LAND OF COCOA AND DYNAMISM

The former Gold Coast and the United Kingdom Trusteeship of Togoland became independent Ghana on March 6, 1957. Although smaller than the United Kingdom, Oregon, or most West African states, it has since attracted more attention than might have been expected for a country of this size, only one-quarter that of Nigeria.

It was, however, the first West African country to be given its independence and, under the dynamic Dr. Nkrumah, became the leader, at least for three years, of the movement for African freedom, even though Liberia, 110 years older, could well have always claimed that title.

Modern Ghana in no way coincides with the realm of ancient Ghana, although ancestors of some of the present peoples probably came from lands once ruled by ancient Ghana. As the Gold Coast, it probably had longer contact with European mariners than any other West African country. This is because of the early attraction of trade in gold, and soon after in slaves. Slight promontories (on which slaving castles were often built beginning in 1481) gave more shelter to anchored sailing ships than other parts of the Guinea coast, except for far more unhealthy estuaries. It also had a highly evolved, if not always admirable, system of government in Ashanti. Under British colonial rule, cocoa farming and mining were much developed, the large, deep water harbor of Takoradi was built and that of Tema begun, and exceptionally fine schools, hospitals, and a university were established.

Ghana of today is a very compact country, within which transportation is relatively easy and quick, especially in the most productive and well populated south. Ghana also has modest tropical temperatures and rainfall, only a quarter of the country receiving over 60 inches annual rainfall, whereas the Accra area has under 30 inches.

The country enjoys the advantages of being the leading producer of cocoa, which the world fortunately regards as a necessary luxury, and which accounts for about two-thirds of the exports by value. It is grown on farms, mostly of about an acre, by some 300,000 African farmers, with as many more seasonal laborers.

Gold has been mined for many centuries, perhaps for a thousand years. Ghana is also an important producer of diamonds by weight, and of manganese. Diamonds, mainly industrial, are being increasingly obtained by Africans. The main manganese mine is the largest in the world, and the ore is of high grade. The Volta River Project will ultimately use vast quantities of local bauxite, only small amounts of which are at present mined, exclusively for export. These minerals, and timber, complete the list of significant exports, but the country may become a leading world producer of aluminum upon the completion of the Volta River Project in the late 1960's.

Thus, Ghana seems to combine the advantages of specialization in cocoa, with diversity of mineral and other production, and is developing fast industrially, especially on an 800-acre industrial estate at the second deep water harbor of Tema and by the implementation of the Volta River Project. The economy is exceptionally buoyant and broad by the standards of Tropical Africa, even the Tropics generally, and minerals have been more important than in any other West African country. The value of Ghana's foreign trade was two-thirds that of the Congo before the latter's dislocation at independence, although the Congo is nearly 10 times larger than Ghana, and far richer in worked minerals. It is not surprising that Ghana, with an annual income per capita of about $200, has a higher standard of living than many other West African or Asian countries.

Nevertheless, Ghana has its full share of problems. Two-thirds of the people are concentrated in the really productive southern third of the country, where cocoa and the minerals are produced. The

Voltaian sandstone rocks, which outcrop over one-half the country, in the center, east-center and northeast, are generally unsuitable for cocoa cultivation and are infertile. The far north has heavily eroded and overpopulated areas whose inhabitants are backward and barely self-sufficient.

In the productive southern third, the oldest cocoa areas around Koforidua have had to be abandoned as cocoa growing areas, because of devastation by swollen shoot; whereas in the southwest, the forest is disappearing in the face of demands for new cocoa and food crop land. Cocoa prices fell considerably in the late 1950's and early 1960's, and there is always the fear that this necessary luxury will become an unnecessary one, or that a substitute will be found. Ghana's great hope for cocoa probably lies in sales to the Communist countries, hitherto exceedingly modest in their purchases.

Gold mining has generally become less profitable. Some companies ceased operations in the late 1950's, and others were bought out by the Ghana Government in 1961, after having been subsidized for a time. The present concentration in a few companies and mines, however, is likely to survive for a long time, since, in particular, the Obuasi mine of Ashanti Goldfields Corporation probably has the richest square mile of gold-bearing ores in the world. In 65 years it has produced around 7.5 million ounces of gold from about the same number of tons of ore, or one-third of all gold produced in Ghana.

The Volta River Project is the main hope for economic advance. It involves the construction of a dam 370 feet high and 2,100 feet long across the Volta river at Akosombo, northeast of Accra, to permit ultimate generation of up to 768,000 kilowatts, most of which will be used to produce about 135,000 tons of aluminum. Electric power will also be available for many towns and for the existing mines at cheaper rates than now, and may later be used at a ferro-manganese plant and iron smelter using iron ores from the Shiene Hills, near an arm of the future lake.

This will cover 3,275 square miles (nearly 4 per cent of Ghana) and be the largest man-made lake in the world. Fortunately, it will submerge only poor lands of the Voltaian sandstone country, and require resettlement of no more than 67,000 people. It should cheapen transportation to the poor north, provide up to 10,000 tons of fish annually to people far from the sea, and enable rice cultivation in 650 square miles of seasonally flooded lakeside areas.

The power development, costing $197.5 million, is being undertaken with American, British, and Ghana Government loans. The aluminum smelter, costing $280 million, is being financed by an American consortium under the leadership of Kaiser Aluminum and Chemical Corporation, in association with Reynolds Metals, the Aluminum Company of America, and Olin Mathieson. The last is the dominant partner in the Fria alumina plant in Guinea, whereas Reynolds and Kaiser were associated with the Boké aluminum project and Kassa bauxite working in Guinea. It is possible, therefore, that Ghana may initially import Guinea alumina.

Ghana would have preferred to use her own bauxite and make alumina from the start, but this part of the original Volta River Project has been dropped, together with the ancillary works they would have required (such as railroads) to save initial costs. However, such developments are likely in the 1970's, as well as smaller supplementary power stations nearby at Kpong, and far upstream in northwest Ghana at Bui, the latter to be built by Russia.

The Volta River Project is of outstanding dimensions, the greatest West Africa has ever known, and it may make Ghana into a leading aluminum producer. The project will certainly transform the geography and economy of Ghana.

The project was first thought of in 1924, and has been developed as a government scheme since Dr. Nkrumah was first elected in 1951, after having included the idea in his first election manifesto. It was thoroughly examined by a Preparatory Commission that reported in 1956. Unfortunately, that moment was financially unpropitious, world demand for aluminum being temporarily outstripped by production capacity. In 1957, Dr. Nkrumah roused

President Eisenhower's interest, the project was reappraised and modified by American engineers, and the present scheme adopted. However, up to December 1961, there was hesitancy in granting a United States Government loan, because of disquiet concerning the restriction of liberties in Ghana, recurrent (if unauthorized) statements about nationalization, and the content of some of Dr. Nkrumah's speeches when in Eastern Europe in mid-1961. Finance for the scheme might otherwise have come earlier and more readily.

Dr. Nkrumah's most ardent wish is the greater unity of Africa. While he was in power in a colony, from 1951-57, this was expressed in enactments against tribalism, by reducing the powers of about 100 chiefs to colorful figureheads, and by playing down the significance of tribes. Since independence, the Ashanti area of the colonial administration has been divided into Brong-Ahafo (comprising the areas conquered by the Ashanti in the past) and Ashanti proper.

With the Ewe he has been less successful. (See Figure 5.) In the plebiscite held in 1956 in the then United Kingdom Trusteeship of Togoland to decide its future, 93,095 votes favored union with the Gold Coast, and 67,492 continued Trusteeship. Union was overwhelmingly favored by peoples in the north and center, who were akin to those in the Gold Coast, but in the south, in Ewe lands, over two-thirds of the votes were for continuing Trusteeship, with the hope of later union with the then French Trusteeship of Togo. The United Nations decided to integrate all British Togoland with the Gold Coast. Significantly, it was in the Ewe districts that dissatisfaction was shown, and since independence these districts have had several disturbances. At the Referendum concerning a Republican constitution and Dr. Nkrumah's candidacy for the presidency, there were heavy majorities in favor of these everywhere in Ghana, except, again, in South Anlo and Ho West. Since Ghana incorporated British Togoland and, perhaps, most of the Ewe, Dr. Nkrumah has claimed ex-French Togo. The President of Togo (ex-French) has also claimed ex-British Togoland, a claim which has more historical basis, since if this were united it would reconstitute the Togo of pre-1914, none of which ever formed part of the Gold Coast.

On the other side of Ghana, beyond its southwestern boundary, Dr. Nkrumah has claimed the Sanwi area of the Ivory Coast, its people being akin to the Nzima, of which Dr. Nkrumah himself is one. In the Togo and Nzima claims, Dr. Nkrumah seems to be using partly tribal arguments to justify his wider aim of Pan-African political unity.

The decision, taken in 1958, and implemented in 1960, to create a republic, was primarily to prove complete independence. So long as there was a Queen of Ghana, foreign ambassadors were accredited to her and were received by the Governor-General, and Ghanaian ambassadors had to receive their appointment through her. Likewise, the albeit precipitate termination of General Alexander's appointment as Chief of Staff of the Ghana Army in the Fall of 1961 was due to surprise from Ghana's friends in the Casablanca bloc that a Britisher should still head the Ghana army.

Pan-Africanism by political unity has been fervently pursued in the Ghana-Guinea Union of 1958, enlarged to the Union of African States with the accession of Mali in 1960. In early 1961, the solidarity of these three with Morocco, the Algerian National Liberation Front, and Egypt, was proclaimed at Casablanca.

Since the independence of the numerous ex-French territories of West Africa in 1960, and of the four times larger and six times more populated Nigeria, Ghana's leadership in the Pan-African movement has been challenged by Nigeria in particular, and generally by the Monrovia countries.

In 1961-62, Dr. Nkrumah was conscious of the challenge. He sought to keep his leadership by his strong line among the Neutralist states at Belgrade. In West Africa he wooed the Upper Volta in the hope of enticing her out of the Benin-Sahel Entente that encircles Ghana, and into the Ghana-Guinea-Mali Union that would then encircle the Ivory Coast, and physically join Ghana to its friends. Likewise, Dahomey has also been wooed which, with the Upper Volta and Ghana, encircles Togo, Ghana's old *bête-noir*. The

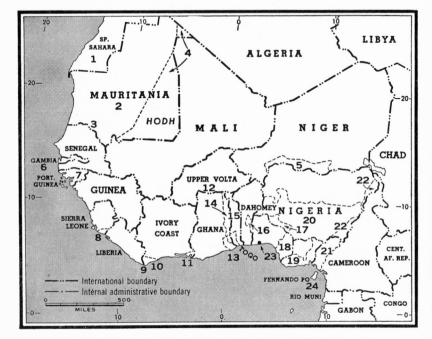

Figure 5 West African Problem Areas (Key to identifying numbers on page 73)

Queen's visit also strengthened Dr. Nkrumah's position, internally and externally, and helped to clinch United States loans for the Volta River Project.

TOGO—AN HISTORICAL INADVERTENCE

Togo is the smallest West African state, half the size of Ohio and two-thirds that of Scotland, with a population of about 1.5 million. The country is the eastern two-thirds of the German colony of Togo, which existed from 1884 to 1914 and was occupied by Franco-British forces in World War I. It was then divided, so that the British held the 32-mile-long coastline and railroads and the French a smaller interior sector. After the Treaty of Versailles, the country was redivided in the reverse way, the British taking a League of Nations Mandate over a small landlocked western third, the French Mandate comprising the capital, coast, and railroads.

---

1. Spanish Sahara claimed by Morocco.
2. Mauritania claimed by Morocco.
3. Southern boundary of Mauritania leaves river within Senegal, and a negro population near north bank within Mauritania.
4. Areas transferred from the then French Sudan (now Mali) to Mauritania in 1944. Hodh a major livestock region.
5. Hausa area of Niger.
6. Gambia may seek association with surrounding Senegal.
7. Portuguese Guinea may be claimed by Senegal or Guinea.
8. Area taken from Liberia in 1885.
9. Boundary gives river to Ivory Coast. Kru people divided.
10. Area taken from Liberia in 1892.
11. Nzima (Sanwi) area claimed by Ghana.
12. Customs-free boundary between Ghana and Upper Volta.
13. Ewe areas of Ghana and Togo.
14. Former U.K. Mandate and Trusteeship of Togo that has been claimed by Republic of Togo.
15. Republic of Togo whose inclusion in or federation with Ghana has been sought by the latter.
16. Yoruba area of Dahomey.
17. Yoruba area of Northern Nigeria.
18. Mid-West State proposed for separation from Western Nigeria.
19. Calabar-Oil Rivers State proposed for separation from Eastern Nigeria.
20. Middle Belt State proposed for separation from Northern Nigeria.
21. Southern Cameroons incorporated in Republic of Cameroon October, 1961, and now known as Western Cameroon. The rest of the Federal Republic of Cameroon is known as Eastern Cameroon.
22. Remaining parts of former U.K. Mandate and Trusteeship of Cameroons became the Sardauna Province of Northern Nigeria on 1 June, 1961.
23. Federal District of Lagos.
24. Spanish Fernando Po heavily dependent upon labor from Eastern Nigeria.

After World War II, the Mandates became Trusteeships, and this gave the Ewe, the largest and most sophisticated people of Togo, the opportunity to make widely known, by personal appearance before the Trusteeship Committee (not allowed before the Mandates Commissions), their intense dissatisfaction at division into two different areas, and rule by two powers with contrasted attitudes and policies. It should be emphasized that the Ewe, like the Ashanti, Fon, and Yoruba, are a people with a long tradition, an evolved society, a high degree of education, and much enterprise. The British encouraged the use of the Ewe language in primary education, the French used their language. The British developed elected local government, the French did not. Togoland under United Kingdom Trusteeship had representatives in the Gold Coast Legislative Assembly from an early date; Togo under French Trusteeship was given an Assembly only in 1946. Until 1956, its powers were small indeed compared with those of the Gold Coast Assembly, but were enlarged in that year because of impending independence in Ghana.

Incorporation of the United Kingdom Trusteeship in independent Ghana in 1957 brought more than half the Ewe within that country, despite the fact that, as seen in the discussion of Ghana, there was a majority in the 1956 plebiscite in Ewe districts for continued United Kingdom Trusteeship. (See Figure 5.) This was in the hope of later union with the French Trusteeship in a larger independent Togo than that which achieved independence in 1960.

The great protagonist of Ewe reunion was Sylvanus Olympio who, born in Lomé in 1902, first went to a German school, then to an English one in 1914, but had to learn French in 1920 when the French took over Lomé. From 1922-25 he was an undergraduate at the London School of Economics. He graduated as a Bachelor of Commerce in 1925, and joined the United Africa Company in 1926, becoming Manager of the Company in Togo before he resigned to lead Ewe reunion in 1950. Thereafter, he was a frequent and eloquent speaker at the United Nations.

From 1939 to 1952 he campaigned for Ewe unity, but then shifted the emphasis to the larger and more viable concept of union of the two Togos. However, this upset many Gold Coast Ewe who preferred the union of British Togoland with the Gold Coast (achieved at independence of Ghana in 1957). After 1958, Olympio was the leader in former French Togo which became the present independent Togo in 1960, but he did not succeed in uniting the Ewe. He was assassinated in an army revolt in early 1963.

The prospect of unity obviously diminished sharply upon the independence of Ghana with half the Ewe, whose separate identity (like that of all other peoples in Ghana), rightly or wrongly, has been played down by Ghana. In 1958 Nkrumah hoped that Olympio, then taking office in French Togo for the first time, would campaign for union with Ghana; this he declined to do in view of Ghana's antagonism since 1956 to Ewe or Togo union. Olympio preferred full independence for French Togo.

In October, 1960, Nkrumah replied by saying that French Togo should become "the seventh Region of Ghana as the only way to achieve reunification of the Ewe." [4] Olympio quickly replied "We don't want full independence and later be sold to another power. We want full independence to be on our own, as Ghana is on her own. It is clear that Nkrumah believed that the only valid formula for unity among West African countries is integration, but I am sorry to say that comrade Nkrumah must realize that the era of territorial expansion is well and truly passed." [5] Since then Dr. Nkrumah has asserted that Togo was planning to invade Ghana and seize former British Togoland, and has reiterated his belief in the future unity of Ghana and Togo (ex-French), whereas Mr. Olympio and his party claimed ex-British Togoland.

The situation had been aggravated by some 5,000 Ewe refugees from Ghana in up-country Togo, and by political refugees from Ghana in Lomé, the Togo capital that adjoins the international boundary. This border was officially closed in 1960. Olympio, however, always advocated customs union, as well as Ewe union

[4] *Ghana Times* (Accra), October 30, 1959.
[5] *Daily Graphic* (Accra), November 2, 1959.

and, had Nkrumah not made his remarks before Togo's independence, Togo might by now have been united with Ghana.

It is not surprising that Togo wishes to retain "our former system of tribes with their chiefs at their head, for we believe that no nation can build a sound and happy future for itself if it does not have its roots in the past." [6] Not only is this contrary to the Ghana view, but to that of the former French rulers and of most modern African leaders, but is refreshingly realistic, especially as the chiefs were supporters of Olympio's opponents. At the same time, he reformed District Councils along democratic lines and gave them greater power. Such decentralization is rare in Africa, as was his efficient yet economical administration.

Like its neighbors, Togo is most developed in the south. Until 1962 revenue came mainly from coffee and cocoa exports. For the former, Togo has been paid greater than world prices by France, which, however, has had to limit purchases, so that the rest has had to be sold at world prices. Indigenous cocoa production is perforce only 1 to 3 per cent that of Ghana (because suitable conditions are confined to the small southwestern area of the Togo Mountains), but Ghana cocoa is smuggled in when Togo prices are higher, and the reverse movement has also occurred.

Since 1961, calcium phosphate deposits have been worked 14 miles from the coast, concentrated, and then shipped from a new pier along the coast. Otherwise, all Togo trade passes through the Lomé pier, off which ocean vessels must anchor. Goods are carried between pier and ships in lighters.

However, "the greatest stumbling block in the way of economic expansion is the currency problem. The Republic of Togoland, although a trust territory and consequently an open door country, has no possibility of free trade with any country outside the Franc Zone; moreover its exports, by means of numerous currency regulations, are canalized to French markets. It is not an easy problem to

[6] Olympio, Sylvanus, "Togo desires close friendship with Germany," *Germany: The Magazine of the Federal Republic* (Neuss Rhine), Vol. V, No. 17, 1960, p.11.

solve, but an independent country worthy of the name cannot tolerate for long the present one way traffic and economic and commercial set-up." [7] Written in early 1959, before independence, this is still the price ex-French states pay in return for high French prices for coffee and cocoa. A customs union with Ghana would still seem the ultimate logical solution.

DAHOMEY—SUCCESSOR OF WEST AFRICA'S LAST SLAVE EXPORTER

Physically similar to Togo, and having also been governed by France until 1960, Dahomey, nevertheless, was quite separately administered, except during the depression of the 1930's. It has developed differently, and the two have had little contact.

Twice as large as Togo, it is thus comparable with Ohio or England (in the strict sense), and has a relatively high population density for ex-French West African states. It has also long enjoyed substantial educational facilities and, like Senegal (and Sierra Leone in ex-British West Africa), has supplied educated administrators to other lands.

After an initial request in 1959 to join the Federation of Mali, it dropped this before the federation was constituted, and became a member of the looser Benin-Sahel Entente. Dahomey is important as the overseas link for the landlocked Niger Republic, via roads from Niamey and from peanut lands just north of the Niger-Nigeria boundary, which converge upon Parakou, the Dahomean railhead. The railroad runs south to Cotonou, commercial center of Dahomey, where a deep-water port is due to open in 1963. This could also be a secondary outlet for the Upper Volta and for Togo, and is likely to be strengthened by extending the railroad from Parakou to the Niger river. Furthermore, Dahomey is also, like Togo in normal times, an important link in road transit between Ghana and Nigeria, although this brings little benefit to Dahomey, and the road needs heavy maintenance.

Old Dahomey was a famous West African state with its capital

[7] Olympio, Sylvanus, "The Republic of Togoland," *Progress* (London), Vol.47, 1959, p.57.

at Abomey, known for its women's battalions, first raised in 1729 for wars against the Yoruba (Nigeria), when men were somewhat depleted in number. The state was notorious for its human sacrifices, and for the supply of military and political prisoners to coastal states for sale to European slave dealers, long centered at Ouidah (Whydah), from which the last Portuguese slave ship sailed in 1885.

Around Abomey are oil-palm plantations, planted by prisoners, and established to provide another income for Dahomey kings when they could no longer sell their prisoners for export as slaves. These plantations now provide Dahomey's sole significant export, and are the only extensive African-owned plantations in West Africa. Unfortunately, most of the trees are very old, have been neglected, and thus yield poorly, but the French established four large palm-oil mills around 1950 to improve the yield and quality of oil. In this they only partly succeeded, because of the poor quality of the fruit. High guaranteed prices are given for the produce, so that Dahomey, like other ex-French West African republics, is still tied to the French market. Good food crops are produced on fertile soils around Abomey, and fish are trapped in permanent wicker nets in the lagoons.

Porto-Novo, a former rival and then vassal to old Dahomey, is the capital on the north side of a lagoon that is navigable to Lagos, Nigeria. Only here, in Mauritania, and Ghana, is the capital other than the chief port.

In Dahomey, the chief port is Cotonou, a mere pier pending the completion of the deep water harbor. This pier, like that at Lomé, and many more formerly along the West-African coast, is so inconvenient and congested that many goods, such as petroleum, are imported via Lagos.

Another link with Nigeria is a Yoruba minority in Dahomey of about 160,000. (See Figure 5.) Dahomey undoubtedly feels overshadowed by Nigeria, and the Benin-Sahel Entente is a valuable consolidating influence, as was exceptionally liberal French aid which, between 1947 and 1957, amounted to $50 million.

THE FEDERATION OF NIGERIA—THE INDIA OF AFRICA?

Last in this survey of the lands of West Africa is the Federation of Nigeria, the greatest of all in its population, diversity—both natural and human—and in the broad base and great promise of its economy.

Nigeria became a united country only in 1914, and 40 years later, in 1954, it became what is more natural to it—a Federation. Independent in 1960, this is West Africa's only Federation, Cameroon being a part of West Central Africa. As far back as 1923, Nigeria was the first British colony to have elected African members of its Legislative Council. It was only its size—and especially the complexity of devising a constitution to suit its very different peoples—that delayed (at the request of some of them) its independence until 1960, three years later than Ghana.

Nigeria is as large as Texas, Arkansas, and Louisiana combined, is the most populated country of Africa, and the fourth so in the British Commonwealth—after India, Pakistan, and the United Kingdom. It is also about the same size as Pakistan, but with only half the latter's population. One in seven of all Africa's peoples is a Nigerian, one in four of those in Africa south of the Sahara, and one in two of West Africans—despite the fact that it occupies only one-seventh the productive area of West Africa.

The Federation's vital statistics are shown in Table 2.

Table 2   *Federation of Nigeria and its Regions by Area and Population*

Region	Capital	Area (square miles)	Population (Censuses)	Population (per square mile)
Northern Nigeria	Kaduna	281,782	16,813,000 (1952)	60
Western Nigeria	Ibadan	45,376	6,087,917 (1952)	134
Eastern Nigeria	Enugu	29,484	7,171,675 (1953)	243
Lagos Federal District	—	27	271,800 (1952)	10,067
Federation of Nigeria	Lagos	356,669	30,425,000 (1952-3)	85

It should be noted that the Northern Nigerian figures include those parts of the former United Kingdom Trusteeship of the Cameroons that chose to join Nigeria in 1961. The Southern Cameroons, of course, are not included, since they voted to join the Republic of Cameroon and are now known as Western Cameroon. (See Figure 5.) It should also be appreciated that, although Nigeria terminated unitary government after 40 years, regionalization so far affords units larger and more populated than many states. Thus, Northern Nigeria exceeds Texas, Western Nigeria exceeds Louisiana, and Eastern Nigeria surpasses West Virginia in both size and population.

Nigeria is West Africa's only country with a really productive savannah or northern area, as well as a forest or southern zone. This is naturally a reflection of its size, and its economic strength. The parts must be understood if the whole is to be appreciated.

Northern Nigeria, nearly four times the combined areas of Western and Eastern Nigeria, is, nevertheless, less densely populated than they are. This is mainly because rainfall is more seasonal, and so agricultural possibilities are far less. Water scarcity also restricts human settlement—particularly in the northwest and northeast. Furthermore, in Nigeria's "Middle Belt," which is Northern Nigeria's southern area, human settlement has been reduced by slave raiding in the past, the later spread of the tsetse fly, and by the narrow range of its agriculture.

North-central Nigeria, however, is well cultivated by Hausa with crops of peanuts (second world area for export), cotton, and tobacco —all for sale; and guinea corn (sorghum) and millet—mainly for food. In the drier areas, nomadic herds of cattle, sheep, and goats are kept by Fulani and, although the cattle are kept primarily for prestige and subsistence, their commercialization is fast increasing, and they provide most of Nigeria's meat supply. Sokoto and Kano goats are prized for their glacé kid leather much appreciated in the United States and Europe. The Jos Plateau is an important producer of tin since before colonial days, and the associated mineral columbite has been worked since World War II. Tin smelting is developing, and diverse industries are centered at Kano, Zaria, and Kaduna. A new "economic frontier" is being opened in the northeast by a long new branch railroad from near Jos to Maiduguri. This will bring on to world markets more peanuts, peanut oil, and cotton, as well as similar produce in transit from the northern tip of Cameroon and southwest Chad. The Middle Belt and the northwest of Nigeria are more difficult areas to develop.

Eastern Nigeria, long dependent upon oil-palm produce for subsistence and for export, has been most fortunate in the discovery and working of oil near Port Harcourt by B. P.—Shell. This may be Nigeria's greatest export by 1970, and has completely changed the economic position of Eastern Nigeria, which was faced with the sharp decline of its coalfield, following dieselization of the Nigerian and Ghana railroads. However, oil, natural gas, and coal that is more suitable for gas and by-product manufacture, are good bases for chemical industries that should come shortly, as may an iron and steel industry using rather poor iron ores near Lokoja, at the confluence of the Niger and Benue rivers.

Meanwhile, Eastern Nigeria sells nearly three-fifths of the world's palm kernels and one-third of the palm oil. There is increased cultivation of cashew nuts and rubber. Mineral-oil output is rising by nearly a million tons a year, and a Port Harcourt refinery will deal with a million tons annually for the Nigerian market. Cement is produced, glass manufacture could be developed, but large-scale lead and zinc mining awaits higher prices. Industries are based mainly at Port Harcourt (situated on the oilfield, and served by the eastern railroad, good roads, and river navigation) and at Enugu (the capital, also well served by roads, the railroad, and on a coalfield).

Industrialization is much needed in Eastern Nigeria to alleviate population pressure in the soil-eroded west, from where many emigrate for work elsewhere in Nigeria, and to Fernando Po.

Western Nigeria, per capita and per square mile, is the richest part of Nigeria. From it comes 15 per cent of the world's cocoa (half that from Ghana), kola nuts for a huge internal market, citrus, rubber, timber, and plywood and veneer. Ibadan, the capital, with a population of half a million and another quarter-million within 30 miles, is the largest town of Tropical Africa. It is a great commercial center, a growing industrial one, and has fine university buildings and a superb teaching hospital.

Finally, the federal capital and district of Lagos is Nigeria's main port and manufacturing center, the vital link overseas not only for Nigeria but also, to some extent, for Dahomey, Niger, Cameroon, and Chad, although some of this transit trade passes through Western Nigeria's delta ports of Burutu, Sapele, and Warri, or Eastern Nigeria's Port Harcourt.

Economic diversity is matched by social variety. Northern Nigeria, in its core northern Emirates (the centers of initial application of Lugard's policy of Indirect Rule in the early years of this century), is strongly Islamic, tightly organized, and conservative. The mainly agricultural Hausa number about 6 million; the Fulani, who are rulers or nomads, about 3 million; and the Kanuri of the northeast (Bornu), about 1.3 million. The Fulani Emirs did not permit Christian missions, except for medical work, and this has kept Northern Nigeria behind Western and Eastern Nigeria in educational advancement, although Northern Nigeria has some compensation in its cultural inheritance from Islam and Arabia.

Here again, the main internal division is between the Islamized or Islam-controlled northern half, and the non-Islamized Middle Belt, the southern part of Northern Nigeria, which has shown separatist tendencies. These have especially arisen among the Birom of the Jos Plateau, and the Tiv who live north and south of the Benue river near Makurdi, who both fear rule by Islamic peoples. A Middle-Belt state has sometimes been demanded, which might include Benue, Plateau, Adamawa, and Niger Provinces, and parts of Illorin, Kabba, Bauchi, and Zaria Provinces. (See Figure 5.) This, however, would be a collection of poor areas exceedingly difficult to administer, and its diverse peoples are very divided on the issue of a Middle-Belt State.

The Yoruba of Illorin and Kabba Divisions in Northern Nigeria have long been a subject of contention between Northern and Western Nigeria. They are divided from their kin in Western Nigeria by the regional boundary, a situation reminiscent of many Central European countries between the wars. Illorin Division was formerly part of Yorubaland and under the Alafin of Oyo, but was frequently in revolt. Ultimately, a local chief in Illorin called in Fulani and Hausa forces from the north to help win independence from Oyo. A Sokoto Fulani established an Emirate in Illorin, like those in Northern Nigeria. This is still the ruling and Islamic authority over half a million people in Illorin Division, 90 per cent of whom are Yoruba and 60 per cent of whom are Islamic; and over 100,000 people in Kabba Division, of whom almost 100 per cent are Yoruba and 60 per cent are Christian. The application of Northern Region Islamic law to non-Islamic peoples is again a major problem.[8]

In Eastern Nigeria, two-thirds of its 7 million people are Ibo, living in the northwestern half of the region. To the southwest live 330,000 Ijaw, themselves divided by the boundary between Eastern Nigeria (250,000) and Western Nigeria (80,000). To their east, and in the southeast, are the more numerous Ibibio (700,000) and Efik (70,000).

Various proposals have been made for the non-Ibo areas, a state for Calabar, Ogoja, and Rivers comprising all non-Ibo areas being the most urged, not only on ethnic grounds but because the Calabar area has not developed as fast as Ibo Port Harcourt. This, however, is due to changes in the direction of trade consequent upon building a railroad to Port Harcourt. Again, such a state (and, even more so, any smaller versions of it) would be very difficult to administer.

In Western Nigeria, two-thirds of the 6 million people are Yoruba,

[8] *Report of the Commission appointed to enquire into the fears of Minorities and the means of allaying them,* (London), Colonial Office, Her Majesty's Stationery Office, *Cmnd* 505, July 1958.

but a quarter of them, living in Benin and Delta Provinces of the southeast, were once in parts of the Kingdom of Benin, and are mostly Edo-speaking. In this area, termed the Mid-West, are smaller non-Edo groups, such as 250,000 Ibo just west of the Niger, 80,000 Ijaw (as mentioned previously) of the southeast, and Itsekiri of Warri who speak a form of Yoruba.

The core of separatist feeling is Benin, but educated Ibo, who have penetrated into Asaba and Aboh Divisions from across the Niger river, are feared because they are likely to take many posts in any new administration. Educated Ibo favor the Mid-West State for this reason; uneducated Ibo would prefer union with Eastern Nigeria. Incidentally, when the Niger bridge is completed at Onitsha, Ibo penetration west of the river is likely to increase. The Ijaw would like to be included within Eastern Nigeria. Thus, a Mid-West State, including all Benin and Delta Provinces, would still include minorities, and a smaller all-Edo state could not compete with the three existing regions. If, however, each of the existing three regions split into two, then an Edo Mid-West might be no worse off than the other new ones (Middle Belt and Calabar-Ogoja-Rivers), although this is small consolation.

The minorities issue was thoroughly examined by the Minorities Commission in 1958, which recommended no change before independence, although it fully recognized many grievances and supported a Development Commission for the Niger Delta to help the poor and divided Ijaw.

The results of the last federal election before independence suggested that only in Asaba and Aboh Divisions (Ibo areas of Western Nigeria) was there strong support locally for boundary revision. Neither the Middle Belt nor the Calabar-Ogoja-Rivers areas emerged clearly; only the Mid-West area really did so. Since independence, the principle of a Mid-West State has been agreed, except in Western Nigeria where strong feelings have been aroused about its implementation.

A further territorial issue is worthy of note, the Federal District of

Lagos. Less than half the size of the District of Columbia, the Federal District of Lagos had to be excluded from Western Nigeria, although it is dominantly a Yoruba city. The Federation clearly needs federal territory for its capital, but it may ultimately have to create a new one in a less contentious area, as did Australia. Lagos has expanded so rapidly, that for proper town planning a further increase in its area is necessary. This could only be at Western Nigeria's expense, and would be hotly contested. Meanwhile, slums are fast developing just across the boundary of the Federal District in Western Nigeria.

The unique range and diversity of Nigeria in West Africa clearly needs a federal political structure, and it is not at all surprising that there are political, social, and economic stresses, all of which tend to occur elsewhere in similarly large areas. Transportation by river, rail, road, and air was mostly built up or planned under the unitary government of 1914-54, but is vital to the several parts. Thus, Northern Nigeria must have access through Western and Eastern Nigeria to and from the sea. Stability also depends upon political dominance (but not dictatorship) by a single ethnic group in each region. So long as opposition is tolerated, the parties of these ethnic groups provide opposition in other regions, and must meet in the federal parliament where, however, the dominant party of Northern Nigeria will always be favored in view of its far greater population. On the other hand, Western and Eastern Nigeria have the vital links overseas.

Dominance of a strongly conservative party and Islamic area, yet the need for concessions to others in a broad policy that will command wide agreement among diverse groups, largely explains Nigerian policy. Internally, it is naturally less centralist, and is not averse to the powers of chiefs. Also, because of the existence, long before colonial days, of widespread internal commerce, which has greatly expanded since, there is a considerable mercantile class, especially in the south. In the north, Arabic culture is widespread, which discourages rash change or demagogy. Leader worship is restrained and less focused in a federation. Education has long been quite widely diffused in Western and Eastern Nigeria, while Islamic traditions are centuries old in Northern Nigeria, so that there is a considerable professional class.

Externally, Nigeria, in view of its own political structure, has naturally favored African integration by technical cooperation, rather than by political unification. It is indeed fortunate that Nigeria's prime minister is on record as saying, ". . . it is not for us to go out to show to the smaller nations that we are big in size and population and therefore they have to come trailing behind us." Such were the words of Sir Abubakar Tafawa Balewa, Federal Prime Minister before and after independence, a northerner and deputy leader of the Northern Peoples Congress, major party in Northern Nigeria, and thus in the federal legislature.

Nigeria may be pushed nearer Ghana's position, as she has in cancelling defense agreements with Britain (which concerned only air-staging rights and training facilities), and by discussions about a republican status for Nigeria strongly urged by Dr. Nnamdi Azikiwe, the rather radical Governor-General from Eastern Nigeria.

The substantial arguments in favor of a republic are the same as for Ghana, but the change would be more difficult in federal Nigeria, because the Queen is also part of regional constitutions. As *The Times* (December 8, 1961) pointed out, ". . . the federal parliament has thus a larger task than merely bringing in legislation whereby (for example) the federal and regional legislatures would act as an electoral college to elect a President every five years on the Indian model. If more than that has to be done all sorts of questions will be raised, as well as the big question whether the President should be no more than an elected constitutional monarch. Sir Abubakar has made it clear that if anything more than an 'Indian' type of federal republic were envisaged it would be necessary to have an elective presidency, which would involve a change towards the true North American presidential system with its division of powers and limitations imposed by states' sovereignty.

The Indian pattern would be easier—but would other African Presidents understand it any better than the British monarchy? They might still doubt if the federal Prime Minister was the real repository of power. It might not suit a Nigerian President either."

The three great regions of Nigeria are well typified in the persons of the Federal Prime Minister from Northern Nigeria, the Governor-General from Eastern Nigeria, and the leader of the federal opposition from Western Nigeria. Nigeria is almost the only West African (indeed one of the few African) state with a sustained opposition. Its significance is emphasized by the size and outstanding population of the country. It will be interesting to see if the federal structure remains democratic, whether Nigeria continues to favor technical rather than political integration in Africa, and whether she retains the high esteem in which she is held in Africa and the World.

The Guinea Coast lands are the economic heart of West Africa. Since the first days of European maritime contact they have gained upon the interior lands, where once-famous states held sway but are now much poorer.

The Guinea Coast lands are most blessed by nature, especially with considerable but not usually excessive rainfall. This has usually permitted the natural growth of valuable timber (still an important export from the Ivory Coast, Ghana, and Western Nigeria), and the cultivation of the far more valuable cocoa, coffee, oil palm, rubber, kola, and citrus and cashew nut trees, which largely account for the cash income of these countries. Only Nigeria also has considerable income accruing from savannah lands. Substantial mineral resources have been exploited, for long in Ghana, but more recently in the Ivory Coast, Togo, and Eastern Nigeria. It is not surprising that with such resources, proximity to the coast, and long contact with Europe, that transportation is relatively well developed in these countries; nor that most of the greatest clusters of population are here, certainly almost all of those with a tolerable standard of living. These lands are also benefiting most from new developments, notably the Volta River Project in Ghana, phosphate mining in Togo, improvement of navigation on the lower Niger, and oil exploitation in Eastern Nigeria, so that the disparity between these lands and those of the dry interior is likely to grow. West Africa's greatest potential is in the Guinea coast lands, followed by those of the southwest coast.

III   *Political Allegiances and Divisions*

Africa, more than any other continent, has been characterized by an immense mosaic of often tiny ethnic groups, a feature as notable for West Africa as for any other division of the continent, as Figure 1 reminds us. The map shows how this original fragmentation has been more accentuated in West Africa than elsewhere in the continent, by the super-imposition of colonial and post-colonial boundaries that enclosed contrasted aims and methods of colonial rule, and their diverse inheritances in very differently organized independent states.

There are three dominant political loyalties in West Africa: to the tribe or nation, going back to pre-colonial days; to the state, emanating from colonial and post-colonial times; and to Pan-Africanism, a reaction to the divisions of pre-colonialism, colonialism, and independence.

The first loyalty was usually called "tribal" by colonial powers, which would elsewhere have called people (such as the Welsh) a "national" group. Where African peoples are sufficiently numerous and organized, there is no reason not to call them national. Those groups that were strongest in pre-colonial times are those still asserting their individuality, for example, the Mauritanians, Mossi, Ashanti, Ewe, Fon (Dahomey), Yoruba, and Ibo. Some were and are nomadic, such as the Mauritanians; some had highly centralized forms of government, such as the Ashanti; and some were more decentralized, such as the Mossi and Yoruba. Some had no chiefs, such as the Ibo.

It is understandable that peoples who have felt aggrieved by the rule of another group should now assert their own claims. Thus, in Nigeria, the Bini have sought a new Region for themselves, apart from the Yoruba; the Ibibio, Efik, and Ijaw in the East from the Ibo; and the Tiv, Birom, and others in the North from the Fulani and Hausa.

Although tribal or national loyalties are strong, especially among the ordinary country folk, they are rarely so extensive as to dominate states, except Mauritania. They usually extend over such small areas as to be virtually impossible as independent states, and are so common as to be no necessarily overwhelming impediment to a wider unity. Tribal loyalties are being minimized by educated Africans, except when such loyalties are useful for political ends. Tribal loyalties are strongest (or allowed to be strongest) in the less radical and more decentralized states, especially those like Nigeria that still tolerate opposition parties. They are least tolerated in such radical and highly centralized states as Ghana, Guinea, and Mali.

It is evident that the importance of tribal or national loyalties is subject to modification according to the nature and stage of state evolution. It is much to be hoped that national cultures can be retained alongside wider state, Pan-African, or international loyalties; just as it would be a pity if the national identity of the Welsh, Scots, or Irish were ever submerged into a thereby infinitely duller British identity.

State consciousness, the second loyalty, is usually the result of the opposition of popular leaders and mass parties to colonial rule, and of independence wholly or mainly within the former colonial boundaries. Within these there is usually one official language, one cultural tradition left by the former ruler, and its administrative, judicial, ecclesiastical, social, and economic systems. Means of transportation, each organized within the boundaries with few international intercolonial links, have likewise encouraged statehood.

Statehood is also the result of educated leaders "playing down" tribalism; of seeking a unified Ghana, for instance, rather than a federal one, which would have given greater power to the Ashanti and others, but would have been costly and difficult to work in a country the size only of Great Britain. Much larger and far more populated Nigeria has needed and been able to afford the cost and complexities of a federal constitution.

The most persuasive factors in encouraging separate independence for the members of the former Federation of French West Africa (and, likewise, that of former French Equatorial Africa) have been not only the dislike of the old centralized structure, but the attractions of a vote at the United Nations, a voice with which to shout for foreign aid, more posts for ministers, ambassadors, and so on.

Outside the Nigerian Federation, statehood has increasingly come to mean one-party rule. In part this is the consequence of colonial conditions, and in part the result of independence. In French West Africa one party was commonly favored by the administration, overtly or not, and whether that party or another party is now in power, one-party rule has been regarded as normal. Moreover, the multiplicity of French political parties, and the instability of coalition governments in France during the whole period of French colonial rule, did not inspire French Africa's leaders with any wish to copy them. Rather, they now distrust all multi-party systems.

In British West Africa violently anti-British parties were ultimately as much tolerated as others. Hence, Dr. Nkrumah, leader of the victorious Convention Peoples Party, was released in 1951 from a prison sentence for sedition, to become Leader of Government Business. Opposition to his policies on the part of Ghanaians in turn come to look like opposition to independence itself. This factor, indeed, is almost universal, and will continue so long as the leaders are those who brought their states to independence, unless there is a fundamental change in political or economic conditions.

There are, furthermore, the natural difficulties in the evolution from colonialism to independence that encourage authoritarian government, the need for a strong and effective administration to ensure that the frail political and economic structures do not break down under the strain of all the new forces and tasks falling upon them. If opposition is allowed from parties, this may develop into opposition from the numerous tribal groups, and to general political collapse. Economic problems are also usually so pressing that political opposition implies dangerous delay.

There are also said to be specifically African factors encouraging one-party rule. The word "opposition" is said to be absent in most African languages; the nearest equivalent is "enemy." Free speech, free assembly, and a free press are also alien to most Africans. They are also said to be more accustomed to leadership by one person (and so to one person leading a politically dominant group), with a more personal, direct, and unhesitant rule. Whatever be the truth or otherwise of these suggestions, the dangers of generalization should also be remembered. Nevertheless, chieftainship was and is a normal characteristic, which very much explains one-party rule under modern political conditions in Africa.

Authoritarian rule is by no means exclusively African; it is in fact widespread in Central and South America, Asia, and parts of Europe. Democracy is the rare and tender plant, which evolved very slowly and relatively recently where it now flourishes, and cannot be simply transplanted.

Discussion, however, is, and always has been, a characteristic of African political life. It has an important place in tribal councils, trade unions, and in political party committees. Although one-party rule may be almost universal in unitary states, the ruling party usually has several political wings or sections within it.

The different socio-political and economic circumstances of Africa, and the recently rapid evolution to independence of countries with weak preindustrialized economies, also make it wholly unrealistic to suppose that Democracy can be exported without severe changes. Moreover, it has been endangered by encouraging the letter as well as the spirit. This is especially true of the British, who have sought to transplant the rules and trappings of Westminster to their colonies. It was rather absurd to see the Speaker of the Ghana

Assembly in breeches and wig preceded by a mace, in a country with far more appropriate symbols. It is altogether laudable that these were substituted when the republic was proclaimed in 1960. West African states must evolve their own structures and philosophies, with roots in their own traditions, and with the equipment for rapid development within the world, parts of which are evolving even faster economically, for example, the United States, Russia, and China.

Size and large populations plainly have economic advantages in the modern world, and the merits of such groupings in Africa are obvious. It is such thoughts and fellow feelings toward other Africans that impel Pan-Africanism, the third political loyalty of West Africans. Pan-Africanism, far stronger than its counterparts in the equally once all-colonial Americas, or once partly colonial Asia, is expressed in diverse ways politically and philosophically.

The latter has found its most eminent exponent in Leopold Senghor, poet, politician, and now President of Senegal. It is he who in the 1930's launched the idea of *Negritude*, a defense of African culture against French Assimilation. In a lecture at Oxford, when on an official visit to Britain in October 1961, he described Negritude as "the whole complex of civilised values—cultural, economic, social and political—which characterise the black peoples, or, more precisely, the Negro-African world. . . . The sense of communion, the gift of myth-making, the gift of rhythm, such are the essential elements of Negritude." African, and particularly West African, culture has also been much advanced through the publications of journals and books by *Présence Africaine*, a cooperative African publishing house in Paris.

Another philosophical conception is that of the *African Personality*, a concept often mentioned by Dr. Nkrumah. Sometimes it seems a personal attribute—a reaction from European culture and ideas; sometimes an impersonal one—as when Ghana Airways have been said to be a means of "projecting the African Personality"; or a diplomatic conception linked with Neutralism and a Monroe Doctrine for Africa.

Politically, Pan-Africanism is expressed in two main ways. The first of these is the approach to African unity through political unity. This is the view of the Casablanca states, so-called from the Casablanca Conference of January, 1961. Conference resolutions, and the various Committees set up, are very similar to those of the Monrovia states. The outstanding differences relevant to West Africa are the Casablanca states' opposition to bases (such as the French naval one at Dakar), to defense agreements between West African states and non-African states (such as the American-Liberian one), and especially to French policy in Algeria until 1962. This latter point has especially separated the Casablanca states from the ex-French states of the Monrovia group which, although sympathetic to the Algerians, were unwilling to criticize France openly, probably because so many of them are vitally dependent upon French aid or have French bases. In West Africa the Casablanca states are Ghana, Guinea, and Mali, linked in their Union of African States.

The Monrovia states, so named from the Monrovia Conference of May, 1961, include the ex-French Brazzaville states (named after their conference of December, 1960) and the English speaking states of Liberia, Sierra Leone, Nigeria, and most other African states. These countries, although neutral, are more certainly pro-Western and will sometimes permit bases and retain defense agreements with former rulers and others; the ex-French states have always been associated with the European Economic Community. The Monrovia states very much believe that African unity is best attained, initially, by technical cooperation, rather than by political action. This view is represented in West Africa by all the independent countries except the Casablanca trio. Four of the Monrovia states, the Ivory Coast, Upper Volta, Niger, and Dahomey are pursuing their methods in the Benin-Sahel Entente. It will be useful to examine the Union of African States and the Benin-Sahel Entente as West African examples of the two approaches.

THE UNION OF AFRICAN STATES

This "Union" became effective on July 1, 1961, and was a development of the late-1958 Ghana-Guinea Union, joined in late-1960 by Mali. It is regarded by its members as the nucleus of the United States of Africa, and is open to other states or federations accepting its aims. Among these are the furtherance of the Casablanca resolutions, the pooling of resources, the liquidation of colonialism in all forms, the harmonizing of foreign policy, joint defense, common directives relating to economic planning, and the rehabilitation of African culture.

Although called a Union, little or nothing seems to have been unified, and the Union is, so far, really an Association grouping West Africa's radicals. That it has so far not noticeably changed the three member states is largely due to the fact that they have two official languages (English and French), three currencies (Ghana Pound, Guinea Franc, and Mali Franc), different constitutions and administrative methods, varying relationships with their former rulers, and are partly non-contiguous—Ghana being separated from the continguous Guinea and Mali. As Figure 6 shows, communications are cumbersome and costly across the Upper Volta between Ghana and Mali, and across the Ivory Coast between Ghana and Guinea. Even between the contiguous Guinea and Mali, roads are poor, and the river Niger difficult to navigate, whereas the Mali capital (Bamako) and the Guinea capital and port (Conakry) are separated by the deeply dissected Fouta Djallon tableland, crossed by roads much subject to washouts, and by a steeply graded low-capacity railroad in need of repair. Air communications are available but still costly and time-consuming.

On the other hand, the Union has considerable merits and potential. It may develop a common market of 14 million people, and its exports are largely non-competitive. Mali is primarily a producer of peanuts, cotton, rice, cattle, and river fish; Ghana's main exports are cocoa, manganese, gold, diamonds, and timber; those of Guinea are coffee, bananas, iron, bauxite, alumina, and

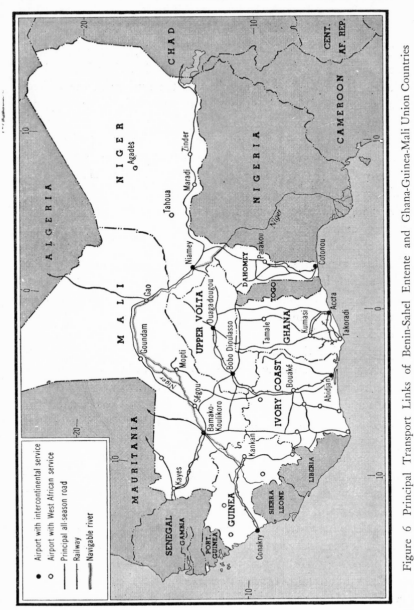

diamonds. Only diamonds are important in more than one country. Mali's cattle and dried river fish have always been purchased in considerable quantities by Ghana, and it might be possible to use Guinea's alumina in Ghana. Politically, the Union is of major interest as the first link across the old colonial boundaries, between two ex-French states and an ex-British one.

THE BENIN-SAHEL ENTENTE

Established May 29, 1959, the Benin-Sahel Entente loosely links the Ivory Coast, the Upper Volta, Niger, and Dahomey. These republics have similar constitutions, identical electoral procedures, election dates, military organizations, administrations, one official language, and one currency. There is a Solidarity Fund for mutual assistance into which each state pays 10 per cent of its revenue and from which Niger, Dahomey, and the Upper Volta each receive five-sixteenths annually, and the Ivory Coast one-sixteenth. The fund will also guarantee loans, and there is close coordination of development plans, policies concerning taxation, public administration, labor legislation, public works, transportation, and communications. The Entente comprises a market of 12.5 million people—1.5 million fewer and with a lower standard of living than those in the Ghana-Guinea-Mali Union of African States.

Even before the Entente, pairs of its states had had long and close contacts. Laborers from the Upper Volta work on Ivory Coast coffee and cocoa farms, while the Ivory Coast railroad and port of Abidjan are vital to the overseas trade of the Upper Volta. The Niger is likewise closely linked with Dahomey through the latter's railroad and port of Cotonou; the more so because through the *Operation Hirondelle,* exports from the Maradi-Zinder areas must mainly pass through Dahomey rather than by the shorter but foreign route across Nigeria. Niger laborers also work in Dahomey, although in much smaller numbers than Upper Volta laborers who work in the Ivory Coast.

Again, there is economic diversity in production: the Ivory Coast is mainly a producer of coffee, cocoa, bananas, timber, and diamonds; the Upper Volta of peanuts; the Niger also of peanuts, cattle, hides, and skins; and Dahomey of oil-palm produce. Abidjan, in the Ivory Coast, is the sole significant industrial center, unlike the several centers in the Ghana-Guinea-Mali Union. Diversity of production is also less than in the latter, and the duplication of peanut production more serious; but these disadvantages are more than offset by the contiguity of the four Entente states and their closer economic integration.

Politically, the Entente is an experiment in *parallelism,* a counter to the richer Ghana that it surrounds, and to Nigeria that it partly adjoins. Were the Upper Volta to leave the Benin-Sahel Entente and join the Union of African States, these respective positions would be broadly reversed, and the Ivory Coast surrounded. The Union's members would then be contiguous and more integration would be possible, but they would still be much less closely knitted by road and rail transport than are the Entente republics. The graver difficulties of different languages, administrative methods, currency, and so on, would also continue.

Integration within the Entente is plainly greater than within the Union. The difficulties have admittedly been less in the Entente, because of common origins, one official language, similar organization, contiguity, and the absence of such severe dislocations as Guinea's isolation in 1958, and Mali's separation from Senegal in 1960. Nevertheless, quiet cooperation seems to have achieved much for the Entente and for the Monrovia thesis on Pan-Africanism through technical cooperation.

In early 1962, the Casablanca states decided at the last moment against attending the Lagos Conference of the Monrovia countries. However, after the conference, a chance appeared for rapprochement between the West African members of both groups. A "Benin Union" was discussed, which could cut across the other groupings. Talks were held to investigate the possibilities of an economic union between Nigeria, Dahomey, and Togo in the first place, with Ghana and Niger coming in later. This could be contemplated because Dr. Nkrumah, although still devoted to political union, had stated that "no one seeks a revision of present boundaries unnecessarily."

Freer trade between these countries would be most helpful. Niger is an important supplier of cattle to Nigeria, while some of Niger's peanuts, hides, and skins pass through Nigeria in transit. Niger and Nigeria export cattle to Ghana, and Dahomey and Togo are important for their transit. Dahomey is anxious to sell her dried fish and smoked lagoon fish to Ghana, in exchange for manufactured goods, including those of British origin that Dahomey otherwise has little chance to buy. Togo would also like to re-open fully the Ghana-Togo boundary for the same reasons, and to resume sales of manioc (cassava) produce and other foodstuffs to Ghana. The latter and Nigeria hope to resume use of the good coastal road between them, which runs through Togo and Dahomey, but which was closed at the Ghana-Togo boundary from 1960-63.

Few other steps toward cooperation or unity have been taken in West Africa, unless one includes the incorporation of the former United Kingdom Trusteeship of Togoland in Ghana (which divided the Ewe but united other peoples), and that of the former British Southern Cameroons in the Republic of Cameroon, which lies outside the scope of this book.

In its first years of independence, West Africa is gravely divided into undersized or underpopulated states, almost all of which are non-viable in a world in which size and large populations are all important. Thus, Togo is merely twice the size of tiny Belgium, Sierra Leone 2.5 times, and Dahomey 3.5 times. Dr. Nkrumah has given the figure of 3 million as the lowest desirable minimum population for a state. If that figure be accepted, Dahomey, Togo, Liberia, Sierra Leone, Guinea, and Mauritania have too few people. Indeed, Mauritania has under one million of mostly nomadic people, and Togo less than 1.5 million in this, West Africa's smallest state. Survival will depend upon aid, obtained by begging or blackmail, from the West, the Communist countries, or, preferably, from both (as in Guinea), as well as from international agencies. Plainly, there is danger of an excessive and long-standing dependence upon aid, which might mean a kind of "Aid-Colonialism" dividing West Africa and Africa generally into blocs according to the source of this vital aid. Furthermore, as Dr. Nkrumah pointed out, small or thinly peopled African states might be tempted, or possibly forced, to make alliances outside Africa, so that a world war could start in Africa.

Such dangers lead to Dr. Nkrumah's conclusion, and that of his Casablanca friends, that only political union can overcome Balkanization, and that political union must precede other forms of cooperation because of the dangers of the present divisions. Moreover, only political unity can bring complete and real economic integration.

Yet political unity has not been achieved even between the contiguous Casablanca states of Guinea and Mali, and boundaries are becoming more incisively divisive and obstructive than ever they were in colonial days. Although cooperation on the grand scale is so much desired, administrative regulations are making it ever more difficult to achieve in day-to-day matters.

In West Africa, as in Africa as a whole, cooperation cannot take place until divisions between groups of states are lessened. Yet the Casablanca-Monrovia groups have never prevented cross-consultations by individual members. Increasing economic links, such as the Ghana-Upper Volta Customs Union, and the use of the Ivory Coast for Mali overseas trade, give hope for more general collaboration, especially now that the thorny issue of Algeria has been removed.

Pan-Africanism by either road may well be arduous but, so far as West Africa is concerned, it ought to be possible to deepen collaboration within the Ghana-Guinea-Mali Union, and within the Benin-Sahel Entente, and to bridge the gap between them. New groupings may also emerge. Advance in the modern world demands wider politico-economic groupings, be they Unions, Ententes, Federations, or Confederations.

IV · *Economic Problems and Development*

D<small>ESPITE THE</small> growing importance of mining, industry, and commerce, agriculture is and will long remain the main activity in West Africa. Fully 75 per cent of the people are engaged in it, and agricultural produce is dominant in all internal and external commerce, except in Mauritania, Sierra Leone, and, perhaps, Liberia.

AGRICULTURE

As in all tropic lands, nature is more compelling and man usually less efficient in dealing with his environment than in temperate lands. Nature thus exerts a powerful influence in West Africa upon the possibilities and speed of agricultural development.

Since it is everywhere warm enough for plant growth, it is the amount, seasonal distribution, length of rainy season, and reliability and effectiveness of rainfall that mainly determine plant growth. Manioc (cassava), yams, maize, and tree crops are dominant along the southern or Guinea coast and inland to about 8°N, wherever there is an Equatorial type of climate, with rain in every month and two maxima. On the southwestern coast, from the Gambia estuary to Cape Palmas (Liberia), where there are monsoonal conditions with one very great rainy season and one dry one, rice and tree crops prevail, although the latter are less varied and successful than in the first zone. Elsewhere, one less rainy season is succeeded by one dry season, the former becoming shorter and the latter longer as one proceeds inland. Seaward—sorghum (Guinea corn), manioc, yams, and groundnuts are important; inland—millet, peanuts and, sometimes, cotton are significant. About 18°N is the limit of cultivation without irrigation. North of 14°N livestock herding becomes progressively more important than cropping, and the two are virtually exclusive occupations.

Soils are by nature mediocre because of severe leaching in the areas of heaviest rainfall, particularly where the forest cover has been thinned, as in Eastern Nigeria; or in the monsoonal areas where rainfall is most violent and destructive, as in Liberia, Sierra Leone, and Guinea. In these areas, lateritic exposures are widespread. The best soils are in the southern Ivory Coast and Ghana—where forest cover has been fairly well preserved, in the *Terre de Barre*—a narrow clay belt near the coast in Togo and Dahomey, in Yorubaland—the west-central part of Western Nigeria, and in alluvial lands along the rivers. However, the latter are little occupied south of about 14°N, because of the danger from malarial and yellow-fever carrying mosquitoes, and tsetse and simulium flies.

Whereas soils have been much improved by man in many temperate areas, the already-poor West African ones are mostly getting poorer, because as population pressure develops and fallows diminish, the intensity of land use increases. There is little enrichment by animal manure in the tsetse fly areas south of 14°N, precisely where such addition is most necessary in view of the greater leaching. North of 14°N where large cattle are found, they are not kept on farms where their manure might help, but are transhumant. Artificial fertilizers are imported, except in Senegal and Togo where phosphate exploitation is very recent. Their use is difficult among mainly illiterate and very poor farmers.

Only around the cities of Northern Nigeria, in the small Lama-Kara District of northeastern Togo, and in small vegetable plots near large towns like Dakar, Abidjan, Accra, Lagos, and Ibadan is there some permanent cultivation. In the first example at least, this depends upon the use of human excreta collected in the cities, whereas the Kabrai people in the Lama-Kara District use mainly animal and poultry manure. Although permanent cropping is widespread in the Asian Tropics, it is rare in Africa. Its successful development would be one of the greatest boons Africa could know.

In the original farming system, vegetation is partly or wholly cleared to provide cultivable plots, often very small in the forested areas and larger in savannah ones. When after some years fertility falls, the plot is allowed to revert to bush, and new patches are cleared. This system of fallow farming is still widespread in all the tropics; it is a natural and simple practice that limits erosion because of the surrounding forest, tall trees that remain in the plots, and intercropping. But it degrades forest, wastes land and labor, and gives poor returns for much effort.

Allied to it is communal land tenure whereby land is held for the community in the name of the chief, who periodically reallocates land according to family needs. Land may be held by a family for decades, but only the crops are privately owned. There is rigid sexual division of labor, varying from people to people, some attach religious significance to certain trees, some foods are taboo, and certain crops are grown more by particular peoples than by others. These indigenous systems worked well in a closed community, but they are breaking down both in an open economic system and as population pressure increases. Permanent tree crops are especially powerful modifiers of communal land tenure.

Upon the traditional communal land ownership and subsistence fallow farming, a patchy overlay of increasingly individual ownership and more permanent cash cropping has been superimposed, especially if the latter is of tree crops, as it is in the main export crop zones near the coast. Indeed, all important cash crops, except peanuts, are tree crops. Nevertheless, even on the basis of value, self-sufficiency agriculture accounts for between 30 per cent and 50 per cent of production in all the countries of former French West Africa, except Senegal (12 per cent). There is also substantial collection of semi-wild produce for subsistence and export, such as oil-palm fruit (Eastern Nigeria, Sierra Leone) and piassava (Sierra Leone).

The advent of cash cropping hastened acceptance of the concept of individual land ownership, and has caused much land litigation. New crops take up space and time from older crops, that have changed for these reasons and because of new tastes acquired during army service. Yam cultivation is declining in favor of the more prolific and less demanding manioc, while rice is in ever-increasing demand.

Cash cropping is patchy in its development because of the need to be near means of transportation, especially for crops like bananas and peanuts; as well as because of powerful physical determinants, such as the need for deep, fairly rich, and well-drained soils with no pronounced dry season for successful cocoa cultivation.

There are also highly important political factors that have encouraged certain crops and discouraged others. British policy in West Africa was against freehold land grants to non-Africans; hence plantations were unknown in ex-British West Africa, except for scientific experimental purposes. Elsewhere, however, in ex-French West Africa, Portuguese and Spanish Guinea, and Liberia, freehold plantations were freely granted to non-Africans, and crops such as coffee, rubber, and bananas, which are best grown on plantations, could be established. These crops still come overwhelmingly from those lands. Coffee and bananas (as well as other crops) have been much encouraged in the ex-French lands by guaranteed markets at higher than world prices in France, and a guaranteed market in Spain has encouraged Spanish Guinea cocoa, coffee, and bananas. In former French Guinea and the Ivory Coast, coffee and bananas have assumed great importance; whereas across the Ivory Coast boundary in Ghana, cocoa alone is important. There it is grown on small individual farms; coffee and bananas are little cultivated, since commercial production of these crops for export is difficult for small farmers—no plantations were granted to non-Ghanaians by the British, and there are no guaranteed markets at high prices. Thus, the eastern limit of coffee cultivation in the Ivory Coast is the political boundary.

Since independence, however, Nigeria, Ghana, and Sierra Leone have shown their interest in establishing plantations, mainly for bananas and rubber, either with their own nationals or foreigners in charge, to raise the quality of agricultural produce and to diversify production.

Governmental participation in or control of marketing began in ex-British West Africa after World War II with various commodity marketing boards. The system was adopted, with modifications, in ex-French West Africa in the middle or late 1950's. These schemes have aimed at stabilizing prices, and they built up funds in the many years of high prices by paying producers less than the world price. More recently, in times of low prices, they have paid higher than world prices. Although freely criticized, they have been popular among producers, have helped to restrain inflation, and have not discouraged production as forecast. Governmental participation in production and processing, sometimes direct, is much more recent and is becoming common.

Probably the most important economic question facing the countries of West Africa is reform of agricultural production and distribution, given the general importance of agriculture, its indifferent methods, and low productivity. Yet, also given the force of tradition, illiteracy, lack of equipment, the isolation of farmers, their tiny units of production and small amounts marketed, reform of agriculture is exceedingly difficult technically, socially, and politically. Fruitful approaches are to open up roads, encourage individual land ownership, control rural indebtedness, adapt primary education to rural and farming needs, and to establish farmers' cooperatives. The latter will only succeed given some education and honest management.

In view of the difficulties, it is not surprising that many governments seem more inclined to leave traditional farming virtually untouched, and to attempt parallel reforms through plantations and large settlement schemes, such as the Farm Settlement Scheme in Western Nigeria. This is trying to bring a new importance to farming, but whether it will succeed at a reasonable cost is doubtful. Most large schemes have not done so, for example, the *Office du Niger*'s irrigation of the Inland Niger Delta in Mali for peasant settlement. Mechanization has proved costly almost everywhere.

Crop diversification, in theory, is highly desirable to lessen dependence upon a few crops. Yet, in practice, other crops are rarely if ever as profitable as, say, cocoa. However, in Western Nigeria, where cocoa does not flourish south of Abeokuta, kola nuts and citrus fruits have been good replacements; while in Eastern Nigeria cashew nuts are increasingly providing an addition to the oil palm. Markets are difficult to enter, for example, with West African oranges, which often have green patches when thoroughly ripe, as well as many pips. This may suggest more local canning, but it would require scarce capital and techniques. Such local processing is one of the most realistic types of industry.

Agricultural advance also requires new areas of production, through the opening of means of transportation and the control of tsetse, water development, the pioneer spirit, and much more, including freedom of access for all to markets in the European Economic Community and elsewhere, and reasonably stable prices.

The greatest danger is that agriculture—the basic economic activity—may decline, while high-cost industry develops. Most countries need to pay relatively more attention to agriculture, especially to improving what they already grow.

LIVESTOCK KEEPING

Africa alone has the tsetse fly and thus almost no mixed farming. The tsetse may carry a trypanosome, which can quickly kill large cattle and, much more slowly, man. No simple and effective way has yet been found either of eliminating or of controlling this fly. Likewise, no cure has yet been found for the disease (nagana) it causes in animals, especially camels, horses, and cattle. Fly-free areas have been made, but at great expense; and, although inoculations have been developed against the disease, their effectiveness diminishes dangerously after some months. Periodic re-inoculation would theoretically be the answer but, apart from the cost of this on poor livestock, it would be almost impossible to achieve systematically with nomadic cattle and, in any case, the animals build up a resistance to the inoculations. So far, inoculations have proved most useful in enabling cattle to travel safely through tsetse zones to markets for slaughter.

The large cattle most susceptible to the trypanosome carried by the tsetse, therefore, must be kept outside the tsetse zone, that is, north of about 14°N. This is the semi-arid and arid zone, where rainfall is small and highly seasonal, pastures intermittent in time and space, and, except along seasonally flooded watercourses, uniformly poor. To secure the bare minimum of feed from pastures, and to keep away from the tsetse fly which advances with the rains and the developing vegetation, animals and herders must be nomadic. No animal fodder is grown; there would scarcely be time to grow it, given the poverty of pastures.

Nomadic herdsmen here, as elsewhere in Africa, despise crop cultivation. They live from their animals, drawing milk and blood for food, eating meat, and using hides and hair for domestic needs. Cattle are means of subsistence, capital investment, and status symbols. The more the better; quality is of lesser account. Animals are sold only when family events require cash, money must be found for taxes or education, or because the animal is ill or disliked. Animals are not kept for commercial reasons, although their commercialization is growing.

Little profound change in this system is likely in the near future; what can be done is the multiplication of watering points, the inoculation against cattle diseases such as rinderpest, and the inculcation of the elements of selection, breeding, culling, and castration. More slaughter in the tsetse-free areas and transport of meat by air (already done on a small scale) may develop. Cross-breeding with other tropical cattle might be tried; although cross-breeding with temperate zone cattle has failed.

Within the tsetse infested area there are various breeds of small resistant cattle, roughly the size of Labrador dogs. Again, they find their own living on and around farms and villages. These animals might well be selected and improved, since such breeds as the

Ndama of Guinea; the Dwarf Shorthorn of Ghana, Togo, and
Dahomey; and the Muturu of Nigeria produce a good proportion
of meat to bone. Although small and few in number, it is, perhaps,
on these animals that attention should rather be focused. Farmers
should be taught their management, and the rudiments of mixed
farming might more easily evolve with them, rather than in the dry
areas of the large nomadic herdsmen. Sheep and goats, which are
more resistant to the trypanosome, are widespread. Certain goats
in the Sokoto and Kano areas of Northern Nigeria and the Maradi
and Zinder areas of the Niger Republic are in demand for their
glacé kid leather.

MINERALS

There was considerable pre-colonial mining in West Africa.
Gold from Bambouk (south of the upper Senegal river), and from
what is now the Ivory Coast and Ghana, was important for centuries on trans-Saharan caravans, as was salt from the Sahara. Tin
gravels were obtained from past and present river beds on the Jos
Plateau and smelted there. Lead was smelted at Abakaliki in Ogoja
Province, Eastern Nigeria; iron also was smelted in many places.

It was gold that first attracted Europeans to West Africa, but
the slave trade soon became far more important. European mining
dates from 1878, when the working of the banket reefs of Tarkwa
(Ghana) was started.

Mining has an increasingly important part in the economy of
West Africa. It has long been important in ex-British West Africa—
in Ghana, where minerals (gold, manganese, diamonds, and bauxite) represent about one-third of the exports; to a formerly lesser
but now rapidly growing extent in Nigeria (tin, columbite, coal,
and, increasingly, mineral oil and gas); and in Sierra Leone (where
mineral developments date from 1929, and where diamonds are the
leading export, followed by iron ore).

In ex-French West Africa, mining was slower to develop, perhaps because of less intensive prospection and fewer obvious sites,

and more because of the earlier reluctance of French capital to
invest in colonial mining enterprises. But since World War II,
bauxite and iron deposits have been opened in Guinea, phosphates
in Senegal and Togo, diamonds and manganese in the Ivory Coast,
and iron ore in Mauritania. Minerals are of great importance in
Guinea and Mauritania.

Except for a very few mines, gold in Ghana and tin in Northern
Nigeria appear to be rapidly wasting assets. On the other hand,
West Africa is rapidly becoming significant as an iron producer
(Mauritania, Guinea, Sierra Leone, Liberia) and may become so
for bauxite (Guinea, Ghana), alumina (Guinea), aluminum
(Ghana), mineral oil (Nigeria), and phosphates (Senegal and
Togo). West Africa is significant already for diamonds (Guinea,
Sierra Leone, Ivory Coast, Ghana). As Andrew Shonfield has
said, ". . . if an underdeveloped country, not too thickly populated,
were allowed to choose three things that would give it the best
start in life with foreign capital in the second half of the 20th
century, it would surely plump for oil, aluminium, and iron ore." [1]
On his argument, six West-African countries have good prospects.

Nigerian coal has always been worked by the government, and
governmental participation is growing elsewhere. Most mining
has been taken over by the Guinea Government, and unprofitable
gold mines by the government of Ghana. New developments usually have some capital provided by the government of the country
concerned. Operation of, royalties from, and taxation of mining
enterprises are, or soon will be, very important items to Mauritania,
Guinea, Sierra Leone, Liberia, Ghana, and Nigeria (particularly
Eastern Nigeria). Indeed, iron-ore developments are revolutionizing
Mauritania and Liberia, and oil Eastern Nigeria, while bauxite
may do so in Guinea.

Minerals are an important means of diversifying otherwise mainly
agricultural economies; their exploitation helps to teach new skills

[1] Shonfield, Andrew, *The Attack on World Poverty,* London, Chatto &
Windus, 1961, p.72.

and encourages new industries. Yet, due attention must be given to the fact that they are a wasting asset to the local demands for refining and industry, and to just, but not burdensome, royalty and taxation payments. Some of these should be used in reinstating damage to agriculture (as by tin mining on the Jos Plateau) or to rivers (as in Sierra Leone).

FUEL AND POWER

West Africa was for long dependent upon local wood, some imported coal, and wholly imported mineral oil. Wood is still used almost everywhere for cooking. Coal has been mined at Enugu, Eastern Nigeria, since 1915, but is of decreasing importance since the development of petroleum exploitation near Port Harcourt, also in Eastern Nigeria, since 1957. Coal was formerly used on the Nigerian and Ghana railroads and in electrical generation, but diesel oil has mostly supplanted it.

Mineral-oil development in the Niger Delta has been exceedingly difficult and costly, some $200 million having been spent before commercial production started. Oil is conveyed by pipelines to Port Harcourt, where a refinery is to deal with part of the output. It is an all-too-common example of the lack of inter-African planning, that a Ghana refinery at Tema is likely to use Russian oil, rather than the nearby equally suitable Nigerian oil. Although reserves are not comparable with those in the Sahara, Nigerian oil is heavier, and is likely to be Nigeria's leading export by the 1970's. Natural gas is used in electrical generation and is available for industry.

Hydroelectric power potential is very considerable but costly to develop, and local capital is insufficient. Small developments have long existed in Northern Nigeria and Guinea, but major projects are now in progress on the Volta in Ghana and on the Niger in Nigeria. The latter provides for a dam at Kainji above Jebba (where the railroad crosses the Niger river in Northern Nigeria) to be supplemented later by a second dam at Jebba, and by a third on the Kaduna tributary. Power stations on these will supply cheap power for towns and industries from Kano to Lagos. Other projects may follow in Guinea on the Konkouré river, and in Sierra Leone in the Guma valley behind Freetown.

INDUSTRIALIZATION

Before the competition of imported manufactured goods became effective, West Africa had numerous craftsmen who made a wide variety of goods for everyday use with cotton, hair, raphia, leather, wood, metal, and other materials. These crafts have declined greatly, and are now significant only in parts of Nigeria and the inland countries. These survivals are due, in the first case, to the great size of the local market and, in the second, to their remoteness and the cost of imported goods. Far more important now are such modern crafts as automobile and cycle repair, and tailoring and dressmaking (by men).

It is often asserted that the colonial powers restricted industrial development so that their metropolitan industries would not suffer. This was and still is true of the Portuguese and Spanish colonies, but rarely so of the ex-British and ex-French lands. Industrial development in colonies was restricted by such economic phases as world industrial recession after World War I, and again in the Great Depression of the late 1920's and early 1930's. It was likewise hampered by the technology of those days that required coal for steam power; West Africa is deficient in coal, as well as in all other industrial needs. Colonies suffered no worse than their independent tropical counterparts in Central and South America, and Asia. Indeed, West African countries often fared better because of colonial connections.

World War II initiated many changes. French colonies were shut off from supplies from France, and some French firms, whose factories were in enemy hands, migrated to the colonies. Hence, peanut oil extraction received a great impetus in Senegal to provide a vegetable oil substitute for normally imported mineral oil, and French industrialists from Dunkirk and elsewhere set up extraction mills.

Service in the forces enlarged the purchasing power and needs of many Africans, and these were sustained after World War II (unlike World War I) by long continuing prosperity through high prices for West African crops. Local production of consumer goods such as drinks, cigarettes, and textiles became economic propositions in such places as Dakar and Lagos, from where there was ready access to substantial markets.

Processing of local raw materials also became more economic as transportation costs rose heavily, and thus the cost of carrying waste that could be eliminated locally. Peanut shelling and oil extraction became worthwhile in Northern Nigeria, remote as it is from the sea and Europe.

The move toward, and attainment of, independence has led to a great industrial upsurge. In part, this is due to governmental capital assistance to indigenous industrialists, in part to participation in projects with foreign firms, and in part to direct operation of some concerns by governments. Industrialization is a prestige symbol, and the larger the industrial unit the better. Steel mills, hydroelectric power projects, alumina and aluminum plants, and industrial estates are especially sought.

What are really desirable are economic industries (or very nearly so) producing goods of adequate quality, for which there is a ready market, and which require little or no tax relief or tariff protection. They are better still if they diversify the economy, provide work for those really needing it, develop skills, and increase purchasing power, without being burdens on the economy.

Such industries are few in number. Even with tax-relief and tariff protection, many consumer goods are not only more expensive but of poorer quality than imported goods. Markets are small, except in Nigeria, and purchasing power almost uniformly very low, facts that underline the need for fewer tariff boundaries and more inter-African trade. Unfortunately, recent tendencies have been very much in the opposite direction, and each state (even each region in Nigeria) seeks to have the same industries. Industrialization is proceeding without regional specialization.

The most worthwhile industries may be classified as:

1. Those processing local materials for an assured export, for example, vegetable-oil extraction and refining, mineral refining, and rubber and timber processing.

2. Those using local materials to make simple goods for an assured internal market of adequate size and purchasing power, for example, soap, textiles, cement, foodstuff preparation, and leather and rubber goods.

3. Those using light, cheap, or compact imported goods, which are easily processed or assembled to compete with costly transported bulky or fragile imported goods much in demand, for example, bottled and canned drinks, plastic and hollowware, shoes, and truck, cycle, and radio assembly.

4. Those using imported goods that may be increasingly replaced with local produce to make simple goods much in demand, for example, cigarettes and fertilizers.

5. Those using imported goods, as do many manufacturing countries, to produce simple goods normally imported, for example, flour milling.

Apart from industrial estates in ports, and some other towns such as Kano and Ibadan, industrial complexes may develop on the oil, natural gas, coal, lignite, and iron deposits of Eastern Nigeria, and with cheap power from the Niger and Volta schemes.

TRANSPORTATION

Colonial occupation and development largely depended upon transportation, which developed in mutually exclusive areas. Because so much of West Africa (like the rest of Africa) is far from the sea and vital overseas trade, transportation is vital, particularly to the landlocked states of Mali, Upper Volta, and Niger. Since independence, there have been moves toward improving international road and air links. It is also evident that many states regard their own railroads, shipping lines, and airlines as important status symbols, as means of portraying the African Personality and furthering Pan-Africanism.

RIVERS

Reference has already been made to the way the international boundary around the Gambia river divorced it from its natural hinterland, and caused the French to use the inferior Senegal river. The Gambia, although an excellent river and navigable for at least 150 miles by ocean vessels, is little used for the reasons stated.

Although the Senegal and Niger rivers were important routes of European political advance, only the lower Niger in Nigeria, its tributary the Benue, and the rivers and estuaries of Portuguese Guinea are now much used for transport. This is because of the great seasonal variation in depth and navigable extent of most rivers, their rapids, the poor lands through which the Senegal and the upper and middle Niger flow, and the devious course of the Niger across international boundaries separating different currency and trading zones.

Had the Niger flowed directly to the sea, within one state, it might all have been as important as the Nigerian reach, which does have a direct and central course. However, the dam on the Niger above Jebba may improve the navigability of its middle reaches. The Volta dam will make its vast artificial lake useful for transportation to northern Ghana; and the Gambia may at last be used more adequately if the countries of Senegal and Gambia enter into some form of political or economic association, although the Senegal railroad parallels the river and would compete with it.

RAILROADS

These were first built to supplement waterways, or where they were unusable or non-existent. West Africa's first railroad was opened from St. Louis to Dakar in 1884 to supplant navigation of the hazardous Senegal estuary, and to develop Dakar instead of St. Louis. The deficiencies of the Senegal river caused it to be short-circuited by the Dakar-Niger line, finally opened in 1924, which also links the two uppermost navigable reaches of the Niger, separated by rapids below Bamako.

All ex-French West African railroads were intended to link with navigable reaches of the Niger, and have the Niger in their names—the Dakar-Niger already mentioned, the Conakry-Niger, Abidjan-Niger, and Benin-Niger (Dahomey), although the last two do not reach that river. They were part of an integrated river-railroad network, designed as much to secure effective occupation and administration, as economic development.

Each European power sought to drain trade to its own line and port, away from its neighbors. No West African railways cross former Franco-British colonial boundaries, and each power chose different gauges. These factors now make economic cooperation difficult. Rivalries are well seen in the construction of the (then French) Guinea and Sierra Leone railroads. Before either were built, trade was predominantly through Freetown, and the Guinea metre gauge railway (like all ex-French lines) was built across the extremely difficult Fouta Djallon to forestall British penetration to the Upper Niger, and to create a hinterland for the Guinea port of Conakry. A much easier route would have sufficed. As the British were confined to a fairly small hinterland, the Sierra Leone Railway was built with the very narrow gauge of 2′6″ and too near the coast. Both railroads have unsatisfactory routes and little traffic. The Guinea line is being rebuilt with Russian aid, and may be extended to Bamako (Mali).

The extension of the Lagos Railway to Kano, with a branch to Baro on the Niger (of 3′6″ gauges like all other ex-British lines still in existence, except the Sierra Leonean), were also partly ripostes to the French. However, as the British colonies were separated one from the other, there could be no comprehensive inter-territorial plan as in French West Africa. Most British railroads were built for more exclusively economic reasons, to tap oil palm produce in Sierra Leone; develop gold mining along the western line in

Ghana, cocoa along the eastern line, and timber along its central line; cocoa on the Lagos railway and, later, groundnuts in the north; and coal and tin along the eastern Nigerian line.

Difficulties of construction were enormous; surveying was almost impossible in thick forest, and all equipment and much labor had to be imported. Railroads, however, were of great significance in opening up many countries; and were mainly responsible for the massive cultivation of peanuts in western Senegal, for the ability to undertake the Inland Niger Delta Irrigation Scheme for rice and cotton in Mali, for the development of banana and other plantations in Guinea and the Ivory Coast, as well as cocoa and coffee cultivation in the latter, and the other commodities from ex-British areas mentioned above.

Railways were vital until the mid-1930's; they still are for the carriage of minerals, and bulky and low value produce over great distances, for example, peanuts and peanut oil from Northern Nigeria, where a long developmental branch opens in 1963 from near Jos to Maiduguri. The Russians may also build a railway from Kumasi (Ghana) to the Upper Volta, despite the forthcoming waterway behind the Volta dam. A 400-mile line also opens in 1963 in the Mauritanian Sahara between Fort Gouraud and Port Etienne, and a 200-mile line will cross forested Liberia from Mount Nimba to Buchanan; both of these lines will export rich iron ore and both will be remote controlled.

Although public railroads are no more commercial propositions in West Africa than elsewhere, the age of construction for general developmental reasons, or for the evacuation of minerals, is not past. Nor is there a desire to close uneconomic lines; the Sierra Leone and Togo systems were vigorously defended by African governments when European experts suggested their closure.

One might have thought that the 770-mile long Dakar-Niger line would have kept the Mali Federation together; but it did not, despite the fact that alternative routes (through Conakry and Abidjan) are much longer, more difficult, and involve breaks of bulk from road to rail. On the other hand, railways from Western and Eastern Nigeria into Northern Nigeria are both said to be vital to the latter, and to sustaining the Nigerian Federation, although road competition has eroded much traffic. The only general lesson is that some transportation link is vital, and that railroads are essential only for certain traffic.

ROADS

Road transport is usually the main means of transportation, apart from exceptions noted above. Good roads, however, are fully as expensive to build as railways, more expensive to maintain than a railroad track, and are not directly revenue earning. Road transport has become a great African enterprise in ex-British West Africa, even if trucks are rarely well-maintained or economically operated. By its flexibility and pioneering it has done more than any other means of transportation to integrate economies and peoples.

Roads were developed within each former colony with few international links and no thought of West African trunk routes. These are now being developed, with the help of the Economic Commission for Africa, to further inter-African trade.

Meanwhile, road transport has been especially important to the development of Mauritania and Niger—both without public railroads or significant waterways, to the two parts of Senegal linked by the Trans-Gambian Highway, to southeastern Guinea joined by road to the free-port of Monrovia (Liberia), and to the northern parts of Ghana, Togo, and Dahomey, as well as generally in Ghana and Nigeria. And, most remarkable of all, Mali has been able to survive without the Dakar-Niger railroad by truck services to the Ivory Coast or Guinea railroads, although this is not an economic solution and the Dakar-Niger line is being restored in 1963.

AIRWAYS

Air transport came to West Africa almost entirely after World War II, and developed differently in the ex-French and ex-British colonies. In the former, Air France, followed later by two French private companies, created a considerable network with larger aircraft than in the British lands. Because of the federal form of government in the huge French West Africa, there was more movement of personnel, troops, and goods by air than in British West Africa.

Whereas French airlines operated in French West Africa, British airlines ran only inter-continental routes in British West Africa. Internal services were provided by the West African Airways Corporation with financial participation by West African governments and the British Overseas Aircraft Corporation. Ghana withdrew from it at independence, and Ghana, Nigeria, and Sierra Leone now have their own airlines. Although Air France and the French companies continue in West Africa, there are also Air-Mali and Air-Afrique, run by governments of former French West Africa. All lose money but supposedly gain prestige for their governments and advance African collaboration. Some 15 airlines operate to or within West Africa, which is directly linked with all Africa (except East), Europe, Asia, and North and South America.

Internal air services have been of great value to administrators and traders, especially on routes shorter than by surface transport. The Mauritanian services of Air France alone made possible the prospection and early development of the Fort Gouraud iron-ore deposit, and of its export terminal at Port Etienne. There are now some 60 airports in West Africa with regular scheduled services (there have been more), some 16 of which have inter-continental services. West African services have been almost the only easy links between ex-British and ex-French lands, although until recently some neighbors had no direct air links.

PORTS AND SHIPPING

At first all ocean vessels were anchored off-shore and were unloaded by surf boats that took goods to and from beaches, or by lighters working from piers. Most roadsteads or piers are no longer used because deep water harbors have been built. Piers with lighters remain only at Sassandra (Ivory Coast) and Lomé (Togo).

Long breakwaters enclose deep harbors at Dakar, Monrovia, Takoradi, Tema, and Cotonou (opening in 1964); whereas quays have been built in sheltered bays at Port Etienne, Bathurst, Bissau, Conakry, and Freetown. At Lagos the outlet was deepened to admit ocean vessels; at Abidjan, a canal was cut across the sand bar. At both ports there are quays in the lagoon. Burutu, Warri, and Sapele are Niger delta ports, and Port Harcourt is a river port. Like most African coasts, the West African ones are highly inimical to port development, save, perhaps, at Freetown, and vast sums have been put into harbor construction by European countries, African governments, and the United States—the latter for Monrovia's free port.

Overseas shipping has been largely concentrated in some 16 European, American, and Japanese lines. To gain a footing into this trade, and for reasons of prestige, Ghana and Nigeria have established their own shipping lines.

Transportation is highly nationalistic but also helps international integration. The Abidjan-Niger and Benin-Niger railroads have helped the Benin-Sahel Entente, but the apparently vital Dakar-Niger railway could not save the Mali Federation; and the Ghana-Guinea-Mali Union has been hampered by poor transportation links.

INTERNAL COMMERCE

In Chapter 1 reference was made to the old trans-Saharan and complementary internal trade. Although trans-Saharan trade has all but disappeared, internal commerce in West African countries has expanded, even though it tends to be overshadowed by external trade.

The basic exchanges are in commodities produced in one zone but vital to peoples elsewhere. Famous examples are salt from the Sahara, livestock and dried and smoked river fish from the Niger, blankets and leather goods from the dry savannah, yams from the wetter savannah, kola nuts from the forest, and dried and smoked sea fish. The exchange of salt and livestock for kola nuts is of great antiquity. Kola nuts are chewed to assuage thirst, especially by Muslims who abhor alcohol. Kolas are a restorative since they contain caffeine, as well as a sedative since they contain theobromine. The nuts are also social, legal, and religious symbols. Many Africans consume 700 nuts a year, or about 22 lbs.

Most internal commerce is done with trucks belonging to Africans, through such northern markets as Dakar, Bamako, Mopti, Ouagadougou, Niamey, Maradi, Zinder, and Kano, and such southern markets as Bouaké, Kumasi, Abomey, Ibadan, and Onitsha. Nigeria has most internal trade, and the Federal Survey Department has published a map of it. Bulk trading and transportation is done by men (often by Dioula in the Ivory Coast—Upper Volta —Mali trade, and by Hausa in Nigeria). Cattle trading is often done by the Fulani and other nomadic herdsmen direct to the butchers. Small retail trade (except in meat) is controlled by women, who dominate all markets.

Bulk trade in imported goods has been mainly in the hands of large European and Lebanese companies, and small Lebanese traders, many of whom also dealt, originally at any rate, in exports. Foreign firms have been viewed with much suspicion, and the largest are abandoning retailing (except for departmental stores or supermarkets) and are concentrating on wholesale trading or industry. They had already become mere purchasing agents for much of their export produce as a result of the setting up of marketing boards. Thus, the large foreign firms have changed their import and export trades quite fundamentally as the result of political change. They have also registered as local companies, in ex-British West Africa at least, gone into partnership with local people or governments, issued local equity shares, and appointed local people as managers and directors. Markets of many of the new states, however, are so small that they do not justify more than a simple organization; such is the case with Mauritania, the Upper Volta, Niger, Dahomey, and Togo.

EXTERNAL COMMERCE

Reference has been made to the place of large foreign companies in external trade, the establishment of marketing boards, and the need for diversification of exports. Thus over 95 per cent of Gambian exports and 85 per cent of those of Senegal-Mali-Mauritania are peanuts. Cocoa comprises over 60 per cent of exports of Ghana, and rubber and iron almost all of those of Liberia. Coffee forms nearly half those of the Ivory Coast, oil-palm produce the same proportion from Dahomey, and diamonds from Sierra Leone.

Although the place of the United Kingdom in ex-British West African trade has fallen in recent years and was (1961) about 40 per cent for Nigeria, 30 per cent for Ghana, 60 per cent for Sierra Leone, and 35 per cent for the Gambia, the place of France in ex-French West African trade was over 65 per cent in the same year. The ex-French lands are still tied to France by the high guaranteed prices she offers for the main crops. These states also provide heavily protected markets for French exports. Thus, on October 26, 1961, France and the Ivory Coast agreed for five years that France would import 100,000 tons of coffee "at a price fixed each year and always at a level satisfactory to the Ivory Coast, irrespective of world rates." The Ivory Coast undertook to import from France $89.6 million worth of goods.[2] There is a great range of French industries for which trade with ex-French Africa is vital, but there are very few British industries indeed for which ex-British Africa is important, and in which there are almost no tariff preferences for British goods. In consequence, prices have always been lower in ex-British West Africa than in ex-French, and goods more varied in origin.

THE EUROPEAN ECONOMIC COMMUNITY AND WEST AFRICA

The European Economic Community, in aim and structure essentially European, initially associated French West Africa and Togo with the six European members, but Guinea withdrew. The great

[2] As reported in *West Africa,* (London), November 18, 1961, p.1281.

problems are the effects upon Commonwealth West Africa and the Gambia. If their goods are allowed in at much the same rates as those from ex-French West Africa and Togo, the latter states will lose the advantages of early association. If Commonwealth and Gambian goods are not allowed in at much the same rates, they may be adversely affected, especially Nigeria and Ghana.

It is intended that by 1966 there will be:

1. Reduced duties on imports from associated African countries, so that they enter all European Economic Community countries' markets on the same terms as those of their former ruler. This is opening up five more or less new European markets for the associated states, making them less dependent upon France. Although lower prices will prevail than those in the past in France, and there will be less tariff protection against nonassociates than once demanded, there will be other compensations.

2. A common specific external tariff, with duties on bananas and coffee, will especially help the Ivory Coast without hurting ex-British West African countries, which are unimportant producers of these commodities.

3. Duties on cocoa, palm oil, and edible oils. These will also greatly help ex-French West Africa and Togo but, unless they also become associated, would hurt Western Nigeria and Ghana in their cocoa export to the Netherlands and Western Germany; Eastern Nigeria in export of palm oil to Western Germany; Northern Nigeria and the Gambia with their peanut-oil export mainly to the Netherlands.

4. Free entry for oilseeds, hides and skins, rubber, cotton, and minerals, which will help associated states like Senegal, Mauritania, Mali, Upper Volta and Niger, as well as Nigeria and the Gambia.

5. Exports from any European Economic Community member to associated African countries to be subject to the same tariff as those from the former ruler.

6. Eventual free movement of labor.

7. Continued grants from the European Development Fund

for Overseas Countries and Territories of $800 million for 1963-1967, inclusive. For 1958-62 this amounted to $581.5 million, contributors being Germany and France $200 million each; Belgium and the Netherlands $70 million each; Italy $40 million, and Luxemburg $1.5 million. Aid is additional to all other assistance from former rulers (French aid is currently about $42 per annum per capita of the French population) and others. About 50 per cent was spent in ex-French West Africa and Togo, 75 per cent on economic projects, 25 per cent on social ones. The early association of ex-French West Africa and Togo was a great help to them in this respect, Commonwealth West Africa and Gambia naturally not qualifying.

In 1960, 35 per cent of both Ghana and Nigeria's exports were to European Economic Community countries, an amount which for Ghana exceeded her exports to the United Kingdom. Although exports could increase in duty-freed commodities to the advantage of Northern and Eastern Nigeria, it could decrease disastrously for Nigerian and Ghana exports to the European Economic Community of cocoa and vegetable oil.

Commonwealth countries and the Gambia are dependent upon the good nature of the European Economic Community members, and their ex-French African associates, since there is nothing with which to bargain. Neither Ghana nor Nigeria have ever given any duty preference to British goods, so that European Economic Community goods are already allowed free entry. Preference is given for British goods in Sierra Leone and the Gambia, but these markets are very small. Likewise, British preference for Commonwealth produce is 10 per cent for groundnuts and palm kernels, and the low specific one of 30 cents difference on cocoa ($1.96 per cwt. foreign, $1.66 Commonwealth and Colonial—preference 30 cents). These are very different from the formidable tariffs in France and ex-French colonies favoring their mutual trade, additional to the equally formidable system of guaranteed markets in France at higher than world prices.

Ghana has asserted that association with the European Economic

Community would be an unequal partnership to maintain European trade in Africa, to the detriment of African industries; yet the ex-French states are satisfied with their powers to impose duties to protect industries.

Ghana (like Nigeria) has always been free to buy and sell where she pleases, and she has proclaimed her desire to continue doing so. She dislikes very much the close relationships of ex-French West Africa with France in particular and the European Economic Community in general. Ghana urges an African producers "club" for each commodity, and an African Common Market.

AN AFRICAN COMMON MARKET?

Reactions to Colonialism and the European Economic Community, and the development of Pan-Africanism, have stimulated hopes of greater inter-African trade, which would encourage industrialization through larger markets and stimulate regional specialization. However, Africa is mainly a producer of raw materials for industrialized Europe, America, and Japan, so that most trade is external to the continent. This is to its advantage, since many of the articles produced are little needed in Africa (such as cocoa, many minerals, etc.). Also, despite talk of Pan-Africanism, tariff boundaries have tended to grow and inter-African trade to diminish since independence. The percentage of inter-African trade in all foreign trade from 1950-57 was for French West Africa 10.4 per cent, Sierra Leone 2.2 per cent, Ghana 4.2 per cent and Nigeria 1.0 per cent. Although much inter-territorial trade is not recorded, a reasonable assumption is that inter-African trade averages only 10 per cent for the continent.[3] Immediate prospects of an African Common market are poor.

DEVELOPMENT PLANS AND FOREIGN AID

Development Plans, using local public and mostly European and American public aid, have been successively elaborated in all West

[3] *Economic Survey of Africa since 1950,* New York, United Nations, 1959, p. 152. The *Economic Bulletin for Africa,* Addis Ababa, Economic Commission for Africa, has figures for imports.

African countries since World War II. At first, plans were drawn up (or added up) by administrators with little or no idea of economic principles or priorities. There was often an undue proportion of money devoted to social services compared with economic developments necessary to sustain them, and wasteful expense on buildings (especially in French West Africa) and on equipment that could not be economically used or serviced in West Africa.

Independence has accentuated the problems of finance, and the feeling that aid would be better channeled through international organizations. Many states do not know how to use aid, or have the personnel to secure its proper use when they do know. An African Development Institute, however, is being established to help states to formulate and implement development plans.

By itself, financial aid solves nothing. It must be effectively used for the development and organization of resources and people. This demands major economic and social changes.

V *West Africa in the Modern World*

T<small>HE</small> international relationships of West Africa include those with former rulers, with the power blocs, with neutralist states, with states whose political or economic systems interest West Africans, with the rest of Africa, and those with the United Nations and other international organizations.

There were indications that the three states that had become independent of Britain by 1961 would almost certainly remain in the Commonwealth. Nine states (including a former trusteeship) have become independent of France and, although Guinea became so under the worst auspices, Mali also had its differences with France; only Senegal technically remaining within the Community. With the exception of Guinea and Mali, the remaining states have always had good relations with France; these have greatly improved since the Algerian settlement, and there is a possibility that the Community will be re-formed. Algerian independence should also help a rapprochement between the Casablanca and Monrovia states. If ex-British and ex-French Africa could enter into one or more confederations, West Africa might become a world force.

The United States has an immense fund of good will in West Africa because of the origin of the United States and its achievements, the self-denial of American missionaries, its interest in independence movements, massive aid, and acceptance of the neutralism of almost all states.[1] Difficulties arise from racial discrimination

---

[1] An admirable study is *United States Foreign Policy. Africa.* 86th Congress, 1st Session, No.4, October 23, 1959, Washington, D.C., U.S. Government Printing Office.

in the southern United States (which receives wide publicity in Africa) and of African diplomats, and the impressions of the United States ordinary Africans receive from American films. American diplomats should also travel more outside West African towns. These difficulties, however, are relatively minor.

Odd though it may seem to some Americans, the Soviet Union and China are respected in West Africa (mainly in Ghana, Guinea, and Mali) for much the same reasons as the United States. Russian aid is less, but it is granted speedily (though spent more slowly) at low interest rates (2.5 per cent usually) for up to 10 years, repayments may be made in goods such as cocoa that Russia cannot produce, and its impact has been more than its amount would suggest. However, there is little trade with Russia—barter is disliked. In addition, Russia has very few technicians or experts speaking French, English, or any African language, and some of the people she sent to Guinea were unpopular; Guinea requested the recall of the Soviet Ambassador in December, 1961. Most East European countries have granted small credits on the same terms, but their experts face similar difficulties.

China has recently evinced considerable interest in Africa, outdoing the Russians in broadcasts and in visiting delegations. She has given credits to Ghana and Guinea, also rice to the latter and, not unnaturally, is helping to improve rice cultivation there.

It is interesting that it is Ghana, Guinea, and Mali that talk most of keeping the Cold War out of Africa, yet, by being the only states that accept aid from both blocs, they have done most to bring rivalry within their borders. No state accepts aid only from Communist countries. The successor states of French West Africa (other than Guinea and Mali) have said they will not accept aid from Communist countries.

The more radical states of Ghana, Guinea, and Mali, and the radical politicians of the other states, are the most fervent neutralists. Thus, Dr. Azikiwe, Governor-General of Nigeria, has said ". . . it means an independent policy that should not oblige members of the concert either to inherit the prejudices of other nations or to join forces directly or indirectly with any bloc of nations against any other bloc in any war, or to act in such a way and manner as to give the impression that any particular bloc or group of nations is right or wrong in its approach to the solution of international problems." [2]

On the other hand, President Senghor of Senegal has said ". . . we are neither neutral nor uncommitted. We stand for a policy of non-alignment." [3] This is a policy sympathetic to one side but of making no treaty commitment; it is the policy of all other states except, perhaps, Liberia, which has a defense agreement with the United States.

It is natural that other neutralist and non-aligned states should be of interest to West Africa, especially if they are the scenes of vigorous development and interesting experiments. President Tito of Yugoslavia was warmly received in Ghana, which shows the latter is not afraid of annoying Russia and China. Yugoslavia has accorded low interest credits to Ghana, Guinea, and Liberia. India, although she commands wide respect in West Africa as a non-aligned power, is a competitor for aid.

Nearly one-half of West Africa's peoples are Islamic (although they are divided into sects), and Mauritania is officially an Islamic republic. Many West Africans make the Mecca pilgrimage, bringing them into contact with the Arab World. Many hear Islamic missionaries who are indigenous, North African, or Asian, and all West African Muslims have bonds of sympathy with other Muslims. The Arab World has increased greatly its interest in West Africa, but the latter, although especially sympathetic to Algeria, is not particularly interested in the rest of the Arab World, except for Ghana, Guinea, and Mali's association with Morocco, Egypt, and the Sudan.

Since 1956 relations with Israel have developed dramatically. Israel sought the connection to counter Arab influence, and the Arab

[2] Azikiwe, Dr. Nnamdi, *The Future of Pan-Africanism,* London, Nigerian High Commission, 1961, pp.15-16.
[3] Lecture at Chatham House as reported in *The Times,* October 26, 1961.

diplomatic and political boycott. West Africa sought the link be-cause the youthful vigor of Israel's development of a small, poor, and ex-colonial environment could provide many lessons for West Africans. An Israeli shipping company first managed Ghana's ship-ping line, and experts have advised in several states on agriculture, cooperatives, youth work, and so on. Trade has grown fast, and many West Africans who go to Israel for technical training come back with a remarkable sense of vocation. Yet relations with Israel have been criticized, for example, by Northern Nigeria on political and religious grounds.

Relations with the rest of Africa are dominantly political, in view of the paucity of inter-African trade and communications. They are concerned with efforts to end colonialism, and with Pan-Africanism as politically conceived by Ghana, Guinea, and Mali, or pursued at the technical level by the rest. All desire the unity of the Congo, and all hate Apartheid in South Africa. Most states have not recog-nized South Africa, have boycotted trade with the republic, and have not employed her nationals.

When the United Nations was founded, there was only one inde-pendent West African state, Liberia, and only four in all Africa, out of the original 51 founders. By early 1963, membership was 110, with 13 West African states, and 32 from all Africa. Mean-while, the Afro-Asian group had been formed, which now comprises about half the members, and an African group (excluding South Africa) that meets monthly. The proportion of members of the United Nations from the Americas has fallen from over two-fifths to under one-quarter.

The United Nations is held in high esteem in West Africa. Its several bodies have been the means of giving publicity to anti-colonialism, and to independence, especially as the United Nations is in the world's most publicity-conscious country. Membership confers the international hallmark of independence.

Most important, perhaps, the United Nations is an international source of aid and expertise, without the stigma of an ex-ruler or a power bloc. West Africa has received substantial help from the

Technical Assistance Board, World Bank, World Health Organization, Food and Agriculture Organization, United Nations International Children's Emergency Fund, and the Economic Commission for Africa, although such aid falls far short of that from ex-rulers and the United States. The Food and Agriculture Organization and the International Labor Organization have African regional offices in Accra and Lagos, respectively. West Africa has truly established its place in the World, and the World in West Africa.

Bibliography

Books

Austin, Dennis, *West Africa and the Commonwealth,* Harmondsworth, Penguin Books, 1957.

Berg, E., "The Economic Basis of Political Choice in French West Africa," *American Political Science Review,* Vol. 54, 1960, pp. 391-405.

Church, R. J. Harrison, *West Africa,* London, New York, etc., Longmans, 4th Edition, 1963.

Coleman, James S., *Nigeria: Background to Nationalism,* Berkeley, University of California Press, 1958.

Crowder, Michael, *The Story of Nigeria,* London, Faber, 1962.

Davidson, Basil, *Black Mother,* London, Gollancz, 1961.

Easton, Stewart C., *The Twilight of European Colonialism,* New York and San Francisco, Holt, Rinehart, and Winston, 1960; London, Methuen, 1961.

Fage, J. D., *Atlas of African History,* London, E. Arnold, 1958.

Hodgkin, Thomas, *African Political Parties,* Harmondsworth, Penguin Books, 1961.

Legum, Colin, *Pan-Africanism, A Short Political Guide,* London, Pall Mall, 1962.

Mphahlele, Ezekiel, *The African Image,* London, Faber, 1962.

Oliver, Roland, and Fage, J. D., *A Short History of Africa,* Harmondsworth, Penguin Books, 1962.

Petch, G. A., *Economic Development and Modern West Africa,* London, University of London Press, 1962.

Thompson, Virginia, and Adloff, Richard, *French West Africa,* Stamford, Stamford University Press, 1958; London, Allen and Unwin, 1958.

Other Publications

Church, R. J. Harrison, "The Islamic Republic of Mauritania," *Focus,* Vol. XII, 1961.

Kimble, George H. T., "Ghana," *Focus,* Vol. IX, 1959.

Porter, Philip W., "Liberia," *Focus,* Vol. XII, 1961.

Africa Report, published 10 times a year by the African-American Institute, 345 East 46th Street, New York 17. *West Africa,* weekly, and *West African Review,* monthly, published by West African Graphic Co. Ltd., Orbit House, 9 New Fetter Lane, London, E.C.4.

Booklets on the countries of former French West Africa (etc.) are available free from the French Information Service, 972 Fifth Avenue, New York, or French Embassies.

Index

VERMONT COLLEGE
MONTPELIER, VT.

DATE DUE

MR 25 '68			
AP 7			
MY 21 '68			
MR 26 '69			
MY 21 '69			
NO 11 '69			
AP 18 '91			
GAYLORD			PRINTED IN U.S.A.